QUEEN OF THE DESERT

A BIOGRAPHY OF THE FEMALE LAWRENCE OF ARABIA, GERTRUDE BELL

FERGUS MASON

LifeCaps Books
ANAHEIM, CALIFORNIA

www.BookCaps.com

Contents

INTRODUCTION

Yorkshire is the largest county in England, and one of the most varied. It's famous for its scenery – the rugged mountains of the Peak District, the rolling green Dales and coast resorts like Whitby, voted as Britain's best beach. There are also manufacturing areas, and Yorkshire towns played a huge part in the Industrial Revolution in the 18th and 19th centuries. Old aristocratic families built factories on their estates and moved from farming to mining, iron smelting and railway building. They were joined by young entrepreneurs, many of whom were later given titles and joined the aristocracy themselves. One of them was Sir Lowthian Bell, 1st Baronet, whose father, Thomas Bell, had founded one of Yorkshire's most successful iron foundries. Sir Lowthian went on to expand the foundry, develop new techniques for making high quality steel, pioneer steel cable production, oversee the construction of the Forth Bridge (then the longest cantilever span in the world) and open Britain's first commercial aluminum plant. During his life he was also known as Isambard Kingdom Brunel. His reward was a knighthood, a baronetcy and a fortune of over a million pounds – equivalent to nearly $120 million at today's values. From a middle class background the Bell family had risen in two generations to become key figures in Britain's modern industrial aristocracy and they set about turning their position into influence. Sir Lowthian spent 30 years on the town council of Newcastle upon Tyne, and served two terms as mayor. From 1874 to 1880 he was a Member of Parliament for the Liberal Party.[1] His son, Sir Thomas Hugh Bell, was one of the leading figures in the late 19th century railway industry

---

[1] The Liberal Party at the time was in favor of free trade and strongly against state involvement in the economy.

and a reformer who increased wages for his workers. He was also the father of one of the world's most remarkable female adventurers, scholars and diplomats.

Sir Hugh's home was Washington Hall, a large Victorian red brick mansion in the village of Washington. Only five miles south of Newcastle, it was conveniently located for his business interests, which were scattered across northern England. It also had plenty of room to raise a family, and in his early twenties, Sir Hugh set about doing so. His first child, Gertrude Margaret Lowthian Bell, was born in Washington Hall on July 14, 1868. Her middle names commemorated her grandparents.

Gertrude was a striking child, with an oval face and clear green eyes surrounded by a mass of long red hair.1 She was also an inquisitive and active one, who showed great intelligence at a very young age. Unfortunately, tragedy struck early in her life. When she was only three years old, her mother Mary died, three weeks after giving birth to her younger brother Maurice. That was far from a rare event; about five per cent of new mothers died during or shortly after giving birth, usually from hemorrhage or infections.2 The three-week delay between Maurice's birth and Mary's death means she had probably contracted from puerperal pyrexia, an infection usually transmitted by a doctor or midwife who hadn't washed their hands. This usually led to a pelvic abscess, but for many unlucky women it progressed into peritonitis or septicemia; before the development of antibiotics either of those usually led to a miserable, painful death. Hungarian doctor Ignaz Semmelweiss had already shown that higher standards of hygiene by doctors could reduce the risks of childbirth but the medical profession refused to accept his findings until the 1870s; that was too late for Mary Shield Bell.

The upper classes in Victorian England often handed off much of the work of bringing up their children to wet-nurses, nannies and governesses, and fathers in particular didn't tend to be closely involved with their younger offspring. Sir Hugh was an exception, though. He was socially progressive and, unlike the abrasive Sir Lowthian, a warm and friendly man.

After the death of his wife he formed a strong bond with his daughter, one that was to last her whole life. On the other hand he was busy; he spent six days a week in his steel mills, and couldn't give his children all the attention he felt they deserved. As a temporary solution, his sister Ada moved into his new home at Redcar, to run the household and help with Gertrude and Maurice. Ada didn't plan for this to be a permanent solution, however, and with sister Maisie, she began matchmaking for her brother.3

Ada's choice was 22-year-old Florence Olliffe, and over a period of two years, she and Maisie maneuvered the pair together at every opportunity. Their efforts weren't subtle and both Hugh and Florence quickly realized what was happening. At first they resisted the hints; Hugh was reluctant to marry again and Florence, who had grown up in Paris, had doubts about settling in northern England. A real attraction slowly developed between them though, and they married on August 10, 1876.

In addition to being a musician, writer and playwright, Florence was a political activist who took an interest in the lives of her new husband's workers. Her 1907 book At The Works: A Study of a Manufacturing Town, based on 30 years of observations and interviews following workers in Middlesbrough, was one of the most thorough analyses of working-class life in industrial Britain and had a strong influence on early 20th century politics. Florence played the traditional English mother's role in teaching her stepdaughter manners and the rules of society but, recognizing her intelligence, also discussed writing and politics with her. Among the issues Florence was interested in were women's rights. Although she opposed the suffrage movement, which was fighting to give women the right to vote she advocated improving education for girls, which lagged far behind what was available for boys. Her opinions were very different from those of modern feminists, however; she felt that the role of education should be to prepare girls for marriage. It didn't take long for her to realize that her new stepdaughter might be better off following a different course.

Florence's influence probably played a large part in shaping Gertrude's interests. So did her grandfather. Sir Lowthian was a Liberal Member of Parliament during Benjamin Disraeli's second government, and when it came to foreign policy the Liberals disagreed strongly with Disraeli's Conservative Party. It was natural for Sir Lowthian to discuss politics with his son and heir, and young Gertrude spent a lot of time listening to fascinating stories about faraway cultures in places very different from the green English countryside around Washington. Tales of Arab chieftains, the newly opened Suez Canal and the intrigues of the crumbling Ottoman Empire fed her curiosity about the world and Britain's place in it.

CHAPTER 1: A TASTE FOR LEARNING

With her father's wealth and her step-mother's politics there was no question that Gertrude was going to have the best education available. At first she was home-schooled,4 a common choice among the upper classes who could afford to hire private tutors. In 1884 her parents decided it was time for her to go to school and get to know other girls, so she was sent to Queen's College in London.

Queen's College, founded in 1848, was one of the pioneers of female education. In fact it was the first school in the world that awarded academic qualifications to girls. It's an eccentric establishment; located in Harley Street, more famous as the home of London's most exclusive private doctors, its buildings consist of several large town houses joined together. Inside it's a confusing maze of corridors and annexes; it now has over a hundred rooms, and new students are issued maps so they don't get lost. Right from the beginning the school has aimed at giving a broad education. Its academic teaching is to a very high standard, but it has a wide range of other activities too. Unlike most English public schools (In England "public school" means one of the top private schools – the British equivalent of a US public school is a state school) it has always been relaxed about uniforms and the disciplinary code is based around face to face problem solving instead of a strict system of punishments, with the main penalty for infractions being picking up litter during breaks. Similarly, education is promoted for its own sake; good performance isn't regarded as a way to win a prize, but as something that's just worth doing. Since the 1980s it's been a day school only, but before that it had a boardinghouse for girls who came from outside London. Later, Gertrude would board there, but for her first year, she stayed with Florence's parents on Sloane Street – home of the famous Harrods department store.

With its relaxed approach to discipline, Queen's College should have been the ideal environment for a well-motivated, highly intelligent girl like Gertrude Bell. She soon ran into problems, though. First, there was homesickness; she had rarely left Yorkshire before and had never been away from her family. As she slowly adjusted and overcame the dislocation another, more serious issue began to emerge. Most of the other pupils at the school were planning to become governesses – tutors employed by wealthy families to teach their children. They tended to be intelligent, but Gertrude found their worldview conventional and limited. Already frustrated by the few restrictions the school did impose on its pupils, such as the need for a chaperone when visiting London's many museums and galleries (all of which fascinated her) she often let off steam by firing sharp comments at the other girls. Of course, the result of that was predictable.

Having been surrounded by family all her life, the question of whether or not she was popular had never mattered to her before; now she had to face the fact that she wasn't. She also realized, and it was a fact that would have appalled her stepmother, that it didn't really bother her. Another girl might have made an effort to change and fit in. Gertrude went full steam ahead on her own course. Those she trusted began to notice a change in her attitudes, a growing impatience with people she found dull. In her second year, she moved into the boardinghouse and her relations with the other girls improved slightly, but she never really fit in.

Gertrude learned something else at Queen's College: it was possible to be disliked by people she wasn't interested in while still getting credit from those who mattered to her. She might not get on with her fellow pupils, but she was a brilliant student and her teachers were almost in awe of her abilities. At least most of them were. Her places in the class rankings formed a neat series – fourth in ancient history and French, third in geography, second in

English grammar and first (with a perfect 88 marks out of 88) in her favorite subject, English history. There was one exception: scripture class. When a teacher asked her to explain her poor marks in Bible study, compared with her excellence in everything else, her reply was blunt: "I don't believe a word of it." 5 Her grandfather's friends had included Charles Darwin and Thomas Huxley, both reluctant agnostics. Gertrude herself, aged only seventeen, was already an open atheist. In the robustly Christian culture of late Victorian England, and especially in a school founded by an Anglican theologian, that was little short of a scandal.

Gertrude spent two years at Queen's College, leaving the school in the summer of 1886. Now she had to decide what to do with her future. Her teachers wanted her to go to university and had already asked her parents for permission to apply, but this was another area where women's options were quite limited in 19th century Britain. The leading universities, Oxford and Cambridge, had been all-male until very recently. The first women's college at Cambridge was founded in 1869 and the first at Oxford, Lady Margaret Hall, in 1878 (although it didn't take in any students until the following year). The subjects that women could earn a degree in were also restricted, with medicine, law and many subjects regarded as unfeminine being off limits. There was one available choice that appealed to Gertrude, though: history.

In October of 1886 Gertrude enrolled at Lady Margaret Hall for a degree in modern history. The subject fit perfectly with her interests and the curiosity about world affairs she'd picked up from her grandfather; covering the period from the end of the Middle Ages around the 16th century, through the wars that had shaped current politics in the Balkans and the Middle East, it fed and developed her fascination with the Middle East. The experience of the university itself was perhaps more important. Women were still a fairly new feature of the Oxford landscape, and as far as many of the staff and students were concerned, they were far from welcome. Rudeness and open hostility were common, and many of the professors were patronizing to the female students.

Gertrude had already shown she was capable of standing up for herself, and she wasn't intimidated by the frosty atmosphere. In any exchange with fellow students or staff she gave at least as good as she got, and while some people were horrified by her robust arguments, her self-confidence showed clearly. She was quite happy to disagree with the most respected scholars, and it didn't help things that she was usually right. She might have been prickly, however, but she got on far better with the female undergraduates at Oxford than she had with the other girls at Queen's College. Her improved social life didn't distract her from the real business of university, either; she was as academically outstanding at Oxford as she had been at school.

Studying for a degree was a lot less structured than it is now. Instead of a fixed course, with set material to be studied in each term (most English universities don't use semesters; Oxford uses its traditional system of three eight-week terms – Michaelmas, Hilary and

Trinity) over a set number of years, study was based much more on face to face discussions with personal tutors backed up by lectures and reading in the library. That made it easier for gifted students to make faster progress, and Gertrude was certainly gifted. She went to every lecture on history she could squeeze into her timetable, and then spent hours every day in Oxford's world-famous Bodleian Library. A bachelor's degree in history usually took three years to complete. After two years, Gertrude decided she was ready for her final exams, which she sat in May of 1888. Walking out of the exam hall, she said the tests had been "delightful," then went to play tennis.[6]

In the USA, an Honors degree is awarded to students who've done extra, advanced courses or research work. At Oxford and Cambridge, Honors degrees go to the graduates with the best grades. Honors themselves are split into four levels. The lowest level is third class. Next are second class degrees, designated as upper or lower second (usually abbreviated to 2:1 or 2:2). The best students are awarded a first-class degree. Grade inflation means this is a common result now but in the 1880s it took outstanding performance to gain a first-class degree, and at Oxford and Cambridge the standards were even higher. Gertrude Bell was the first woman ever to earn a first class Honors in modern history, and she'd done it in only two years at one of the world's top universities. It was a remarkable achievement.

The young woman who graduated from Oxford in 1888 was an intriguing character. Devoted to her father and always quick to ask his advice when she didn't know something, she was also highly confident in her own abilities and had a slight tendency towards arrogance. When she returned home, her stepmother was split between pride at her academic triumph and horror at her forceful manner. Gertrude often let loose her annoyance at people who held vague ideas; valuing knowledge much more than beliefs or opinions, she once wrote that she was sick of people who started sentences with "I think..." Florence was convinced that nobody would want to marry a woman who was so determined in standing her ground and fighting for her own views. She decided to civilize her occasionally fierce stepdaughter, and bring her around to her own more domesticated form of intellectual work and activism. It would obviously be a struggle, but she was determined to do it. The first step would be a long vacation in Europe.

CHAPTER 2: THE TRAVELER

One big advantage of Gertrude's social class was that her parents had friends and family in many places. Florence's sister Mary Lascelles, for example, was married to the British Minister in Bucharest, Romania. A British Minister was similar to an ambassador but a slightly lower rank, suitable for a minor power like Romania. Gertrude's uncle, Sir Frank Lascelles, was a rising star in the British diplomatic service and would go on to be ambassador to Russia and then Germany.7 For him, Romania was a chance to learn how diplomacy worked in the tangled web of 19th century Europe. At that time, most countries still had royal families and powerful aristocracies, so politics and high society were closely connected. Florence decided that it would do Gertrude good to spend some time learning about that side of life. She got on well with her Aunt Mary, too, so Bucharest was the perfect choice. Gertrude was excited as well; armed with a large new wardrobe of fashionable dresses, the Lascelles' sons escorted her to Romania by way of Paris and Munich.

She spent four months in Bucharest and had a great time, but the results were not what Florence had been expecting. Gertrude loved the formal functions – she had learned to dance at school; then, more enthusiastically, at Oxford – and even taught some of the diplomats and royalty new American dances like the Boston. She also began to build up a new circle of contacts. Florence had probably hoped her stepdaughter would meet a suitable young man with an interest in marriage, but Gertrude was more interested in befriending her intellectual equals. One of her new friends was Charles Hardinge, a talented young diplomatic secretary who worked in the Ottoman capital, Constantinople. Another was Ignatius Valentine Chirol, a British journalist who'd been educated in Germany and France, worked briefly for the

Foreign Office, travelled in the Balkans and Middle East and then got a job as an international correspondent for The Times. Both men were experts on the Ottoman Empire, and Gertrude was quickly becoming one herself.

If Florence had hoped Gertrude would learn her "proper place" in the world, that wasn't going so well either. She was always polite to the foreign royalty she met, but she treated them more or less as equals. In return, they were happy to have long conversations with her about their daily lives. Onlookers were less happy when she told a French government minister – in fluent French - that he didn't understand the spirit of the German people, and Aunt Mary gave her a lecture about why that wasn't acceptable. Biographer Georgina Howell called Gertrude "something of a social hand grenade"8 and there's no doubt that was an accurate description, but Gertrude thought social niceties were far less important than knowledge and logic. The time was coming when she would be proven right.

When Gertrude returned from Bucharest in early 1889, she spent several months at home in Redcar, managing the house while Florence was away on a trip of her own. She did the accounts, organized events for the staff and their wives, and looked after her three younger half-siblings. Then it was time for her "coming out."

The origin of today's cotillion balls, the coming-out of debutantes, was the high point of the London social season. Young women from upper class families would be presented to the sovereign – the aging Queen Victoria, in Gertrude's case – then take part in a series of balls, tea parties, sporting events (polo and the annual Royal Ascot horse racing were always favorites) and other functions. The presentation of eligible young ladies kicked off the social season, which ran from early in the year to just after Royal Ascot in mid-June, and by the end of it most of the debs were expected to have found themselves a suitable fiancé.

Not Gertrude.

She enjoyed the season almost as much as her time in Romania, but when she returned to Redcar she was still very definitely single. Florence had been briefly worried by a mild flirtation between Gertrude and her nephew Billy, who'd just been commissioned into the élite Coldstream Guards regiment, but nothing came of it. It is likely Gertrude just enjoyed her cousin's company, and perhaps also got a thrill from causing a mild scandal. They must have made a striking pair – the attractive, elegantly dressed redhead and the tall young Guards officer in his scarlet tunic – and tongues would certainly have been wagging when they went out in London with Gertrude's chaperones trying vainly to keep up. She also went out with at least one of Billy's fellow officers, and made sure to keep Florence informed by letter. Florence was left increasingly worried by Gertrude's disdain for chaperones.

Of course it's important not to pay too much attention to these mischievous games with social standards. It was expected that young upper class women would be chaperoned around the opposite sex, but while lapses bothered Florence, they weren't really all that serious. The fact is that the Victorians were a lot less prudish than most people now believe. In fact, in the 1930s elderly Victorians often complained that the fun and freedom of their generation had been ruined by "Puritan fanatics" and "Ultra-respectability, the great fetish of modern England".9 Queen Victoria herself, usually pictured as a forbidding elderly woman, was actually an energetic and reforming leader. She was even willing to tackle the myths and taboos around reproduction. When the first anesthetics were developed, most doctors refused to use them for childbirth pains, whether for moral reasons or out of excessive caution. It is likely Victoria was fed up with labor pains after having seven children. When she was about to deliver her eighth she brushed aside medical objections – "We are having this baby, and we are having chloroform." After that it was very hard for a doctor to refuse anesthesia to any expectant mother.

Even the most famous example of Victorian sensitivity seems to be a myth. People make jokes about the Victorians dressing the legs of tables and pianos in frilly skirts, to avoid becoming aroused by their curvaceous shape. It's amusing, and makes a great example of how sex-obsessed and prudish the Victorians were – but there's a problem. Some investigation shows that people in Victorian England were telling those jokes too, but they were telling them about the Yankee middle classes of New England. Were pianos in New England decently dressed? No. The whole thing seems to have started as a prank played on Captain Frederick Marryat, an English writer who had been travelling in the USA collecting material for a critical book on the country.10

So Gertrude's free-spirited ways might have made her stepmother despair of ever finding a husband for her, but in terms of what society thought they probably mattered less than her increasingly outspoken atheism. Politics and religion were two things you weren't supposed to mention in polite company but Gertrude had strong views on both, and she had no hesitation in sharing them.

In 1891, Sir Frank Lascelles, who had distinguished himself in Romania, was transferred to a new post. He became the British Minister to Persia, which still wasn't vital enough to deserve a full ambassador but as a large independent state in the Middle East was a useful balance to the power of the Ottomans.

Diplomacy in Tehran was a delicate job; Britain and Persia had fought a short war from 1856-57, triggered by allegations of an affair between a British diplomat and the Shah's sister-in-law, and Iranian attempts to seize the city of Herat in British-occupied Afghanistan. Now Britain wanted to improve relations with the Shah, and an outstanding diplomat was needed.

When Gertrude heard about her uncle's move she was delighted. Probably hoping for another invitation to visit him, she immediately set out to learn the Persian language and once again, family connections helped her out. Her Aunt Maisie, Sir Hugh's older sister, had married Edward Stanley, 4th Baron of Alderley in 1873. Her new father-in-law was historian Henry Stanley, the 3rd Baron, a convert to Islam who had become the first Muslim member of the House of Lords. The irreligious Gertrude would have had no patience for his conversion, but she was definitely interested in the fact that he spoke both Arabic and Persian, and soon she was taking lessons from him. When the expected invitation from the Lascelles arrived, she was ready to move on to a short course at the London School of Oriental Studies. Six months after Sir Frank moved to Tehran, his daughter Florence accompanied Gertrude on the long train journey southeast, through Germany, Austria, Turkey and the Russian Empire. She was overwhelmed by the feeling that here was her great adventure, in a place where she immediately felt at home.

Gertrude threw herself into life in Tehran with a surge of enthusiasm. She loved the luxury of life in the British Embassy, and the social scene filled with diplomats and local nobility. She was more fascinated than ever by her uncle's work - keeping the peace with the ancient nation of Persia while staying up to date on what was happening across the Persian Gulf, where the Ottoman Empire, officially an ally of Britain but not really trusted, sank slowly into corruption and debt. The Ottomans interested Gertrude, but for the moment, they were a minor interest. Her real passion right now was Persia, and she immersed herself deeply in the culture. Whether it was long rides out into the deserts and mountains, shopping expeditions in the noisy bazaars or long sessions with books of Persian poetry she soaked up information about the land, people and history.

And then, unexpectedly, she met a man. The Honorable Henry Cadogan was a secretary at the embassy, and, like Gertrude, he had a deep interest in Persian culture. Soon he was joining her on her trips around Tehran and into the countryside, and bringing her more books. By this time Gertrude could read and speak Persian quite well, but Henry was better. To close the gap he arranged a teacher for her. When it came to relaxation he was a talented tennis player, another passion she shared. The two quickly became inseparable, and when he proposed to her in July 1892, she happily accepted. Henry was from a good family; his father Frederick was a prominent lawyer and politician and his grandfather, the 3rd Earl Cadogan, had been a Royal Navy admiral and a hero of the Napoleonic wars. As she wrote a letter to her parents to tell them that she was engaged, Gertrude was sure that even Florence would approve.

The reply was a stunning disappointment. Sir Hugh and Florence had made inquiries about Gertrude's new fiancé and the answers they got had set them firmly against a marriage. Henry Cadogan's family might be prominent, but they were far from wealthy. Frederick was almost bankrupt and Henry himself had almost no money. This wasn't snobbery on the Bell's part; their worry was that Henry wouldn't be able to afford to run a house, and they were almost certainly right. Worse, Henry had a gambling problem that ate most of what income he did have.11 The Bells belonged to the sixth richest family in Britain but their actual income wasn't spectacular; most of the money was locked up in investments and trust funds controlled by Sir Lowthian. Gertrude's parents wrote that they couldn't approve of the marriage and asked her to come home as soon as possible. She was heartbroken, but realized that if she married Henry she would basically be asking her father to finance another household as well as his own. That was beyond his income; it wasn't going to work. With her aunt and uncle supporting her parents she had no choice but to return to Redcar. Perhaps, she hoped, Henry could find a better paid job that would make a re-engagement possible. Even that hope was soon to collapse.

A year after Gertrude took the train back to Yorkshire Henry fell in a cold mountain stream during a fishing trip. That icy ducking was blamed when, not long afterwards, he fell ill with pneumonia. In fact, pneumonia is caused by any one of several bacteria or viruses, with the most common being Streptococcus pneumoniae. If Henry already had a mild infection when he fell in the water, and didn't dry off and change clothes immediately, the chill could have depressed his immune system and helped the infection explode into a serious case of pneumonia. Now the disease can usually be treated with antibiotics but the discovery of penicillin was still 35 years in the future. Henry's condition went downhill quickly, and after a short illness he died. It was a savage blow to Gertrude, and its impact never fully left her.

CHAPTER 3: RUSHING INTO PRINT

They might have disapproved of Henry, but Sir Hugh and Florence could see the impact his death had had on Gertrude. The young woman was clearly devastated and had fallen into a lethargic mood that was completely unlike her usual energetic self. Her parents started looking for a way to distract her. She was going to Persian lessons again and helping to run the house but it obviously wasn't enough. Then Florence had an idea. Leafing through the huge stack of letters Gertrude had sent home from Tehran, and the diaries she had kept, Florence suggested Gertrude write a travel book about her experiences. Travel literature was extremely popular in Victorian Britain. For most young members of the upper classes the "Grand Tour" of Europe had been a rite of passage for centuries, but now with the British Empire reaching the peak of its size and power there was a growing appetite for books about more distant lands.

Gertrude herself, sunk in misery, was unenthusiastic. Florence was a published writer though, and had lots of contacts in the industry. She spoke to a London publisher, Bentley & Co, and sent them a proposal for a book. Bentley accepted, making it hard for Gertrude to refuse. Reluctantly she began work on the book, although she wrote to a friend, "I do so loathe people who rush into print and fill the world with their cheap and nasty work."12

Gertrude's lack of interest showed up in the finished book; Persian Pictures was published in 1894 and almost immediately vanished into obscurity. There was one piece of good news: it had been published anonymously, a sign of Gertrude's opposition to the project, so its lack of success wasn't attached to her name. Another positive thing was that it had gotten her writing, even if unsuccessfully, and having written one book it would be easier for her to start a second. Now she started to wonder about translating the work of a favorite poet.

Khwaja Shams-ud-din Mohammed Hafiz, usually known simply as Hafiz, was born in Iran around the year 1315 and became a court poet to the Persian kings.13 A follower of the mystical Sufi variety of Islam, which has often been persecuted for its less harsh interpretation of the religion but has always been popular in Persia, he wrote many love poems as well as verses on philosophy and morality. His work has been popular in Iran ever since. He had been Henry's favorite poet and Gertrude had also taken to reading him. There was no modern English translation of his work, though – the best was a 1770 edition by William Jones. Now Gertrude decided to write a new one.

Poems From The Divan of Hafiz2 was published in 1897 and, unlike Persian Pictures, was an immediate success. Gertrude was now

---

2 In this case "Divan" is Persian for an anthology of poetry, not the modern English word meaning a couch or bed.

fluent enough in Persian to catch the more subtle undertones of poetry as well as the literal meanings of normal conversation, and her free-flowing translation (which could be quite creative at times) made for an enjoyable read. In fact it's still in print, on and off, today. Also, unlike Persian Pictures, it was published under her own name, laying the foundation for later popularity as a travel writer.

The same year the family took a vacation in the picturesque French town of La Grave. Located 5,000 feet above sea level in the French Alps, today La Grave is a favorite spot for extreme skiers. In 1897 it was a popular place to relax, enjoy top quality restaurants and enjoy carriage rides in the surrounding countryside. The Bells had a pleasant time there, staying in a small hotel and walking on the green Alpine meadows. Something in the scenery called to Gertrude, though. She persuaded her father to climb some of the lower mountain peaks with her and then went on some expeditions with local guides. It was a challenge, and she enjoyed it, but instead of satisfying her it only lit a desire to do more. Looking up at the peak of

La Meije, a saw-toothed granite outcrop that towered above the village, she wondered what it would feel like to be standing on top looking down. One day, she promised herself, she would come back and find out.14

CHAPTER 4: AROUND THE WORLD

The Pacific Mail Steamship Company ship SS City of Rio de Janeiro slipped out through the Golden Gate and set course for Honolulu. A 3,500 ton steam-powered liner with an auxiliary three-masted sailing rig, she had been built to run from the east coast of the USA down to her namesake port then refitted in 1881 as a luxury Pacific liner. Now it was early 1898 and as the City of Rio left San Francisco behind Gertrude Bell sprawled in a deck chair beside the rail, a book in her lap, flicking an endless stream of cigarette butts over the side. A tall, cheerful man in his mid-20s leaned against the rail nearby, leafing through a small book. It seemed an unsuitable book for such a confident young man; Manners for Women by Mrs C.E. Humphry, a newly-published etiquette guide for refined young ladies. In fact, he'd only bought it to tease his sister and now, laughing, he read out extracts which particularly amused him as she glared up at him from the deck chair.

Gertrude could afford to travel, and a round-the-world tour was a common experience for the upper classes. She couldn't travel alone, of course, so her younger brother Maurice volunteered himself as a companion. Maurice was a captain in the Yorkshire Regiment but he was able to take extended leave to accompany his sister. It would be the last time; a year later he was in South Africa fighting in the Boer War, and after that he was busy with a military career that led to two bravery awards in the First World War. For now he was free to travel with his sister, and they made the most of it. The two had always got on well; Maurice adored his clever sister, and in turn was popular with the whole family.

Gertrude's previous trips abroad had been quite well chaperoned, even if she'd been able to spend a lot of time with Henry in Tehran. This was different. Sir Hugh and Florence expected Maurice to look after her, of course, but the two saw themselves much more as equals and they were both determined to enjoy themselves as much as possible. Maurice persuaded the ship's captain to let him mark out a golf course on the deck, which must have led to a lot of lost balls but was a big hit with the other passengers.15 Gertrude was surprisingly popular with the other passengers' children and organized games to keep them amused. She had always enjoyed planning fun activities and now it was as big a success as Maurice's hazard-littered golf course. The fun continued all the way round the world and when Gertrude returned to Redcar in June 1898 her mood was better than it had been since Henry's death. Boosted by the experience of traveling so far and so long with no real control over her activities, she was also more confident and self-assured than ever.

In Redcar, back under Florence's supervision, she continued helping out with the running of the house and also worked with the wives of Sir Hugh's Clarence Steelworks in nearby Cleveland. She organized day trips and dances, gave lectures about her travel experiences and listened to those wives who were having domestic problems. The work helped develop her political views and also kept her occupied, but not occupied enough that she had no time for her hobbies and sports. She played golf and tennis – by now she was an excellent player. She hunted, and travelled to Scotland to fish for salmon. Slowly her attention started to turn to France, though. She had a promise to keep.

CHAPTER 5: UP IN THE CLOUDS

La Meije is a sharp-edged wedge of gray rock that's been carved and splintered by millions of years of ice. It's the highest point of a granite ridge that stretches nearly ten miles, running along the south side of the alpine valley that holds the town of La Grave. Surrounded by glaciers and snow-filled hollows the summit is split into five rocky fingers, the main one of which was the last major unconquered peak in the Alps. Nobody managed to climb it until a father and son team of local mountain guides, along with famous French climber Emannuel Boileau de Castennau, finally fought their way up in 1877.[16] Twelve years later only a handful of leading mountaineers had made the ascent, so when Gertrude announced that she was going to climb it, her family and friends told her not to be silly.

Being called silly didn't bother Gertrude. What mattered was that she kept the promise she'd made herself and climbed La Meije. Seeing her determination her friends made more serious efforts to talk her out of it. Valentine Chiron, now Sir Valentine, was one of them.17 Their warnings were sensible; since the family trip in 1897 Gertrude had done no more climbing, and basically was a complete novice. Now she planned to tackle a summit that most of the world's leading mountaineers were still reluctant to approach. It didn't matter; she was undeterred. She arrived back in La Grave in mid-August and looked up the two guides she had worked with before and then told them what she planned. They agreed on the condition that she made some practice climbs first.

On August 25 Gertrude and her two guides, laden with camping gear and ropes, climbed out of La Grave, over the ridge and down towards the Refuge du Châtelleret, a wooden mountain hut two miles south of the summit and over a mile below it. For the next two days they spent their nights in the hut and their days scrambling over the rock and ice that surrounded it. Gertrude quickly learned how to use their equipment. It was simple, because most of the technical aids used by modern climbers simply didn't exist. They had no safety helmets or harnesses, no spiked crampons to strap to their boots and gain grip on ice. There were no karabiners to connect gear, sticht plates or figure-8 descenders to control the slip rates of rope, cams or shaped blocks to use as anchors in the steep rock. If they needed an anchor their only option was a piton, a spike of soft iron with a ring on the end that could be hammered into a crack in the rock. The metal deformed as it was pounded in, giving a better grip, but also making them nearly impossible to remove. Only a limited supply could be carried and they had to be used sparingly. Simple ice axes and hammers for setting pitons were their other gear, along with long manila ropes. The ropes were strong and resistant to the jagged rock, but thicker and heavier than modern nylon and prone to soaking up water that weighed even more. The ropes would be secured to anchors with knots, and if friction was needed to control a descent or support a climber it was created by wrapping the tail of the rope around shoulders and waist. They wore sturdy leather boots with nail-studded soles and, because nobody made mountaineering outfits for women, Gertrude was dressed in tweed riding jacket and a respectable ankle-length skirt. To a 21st century climber, their gear would have looked unbelievably sparse and crude, but it was what was available and in the hands of a competent user it worked. In only two days, Gertrude was well on the way to becoming competent.

Late on August 26 two young Germans, an Englishman called Mr. Turner and his local guide joined them in the hut. Long before dawn next day they began the ascent to the peak of La Meije, with the Germans a little ahead of the other five. At first they scrambled over silt and crushed rock laid down 20,000 years earlier at the end of the last ice age – it was better to do this stage in the dark, Gertrude wrote to her father, because it was boring - then came to the foot of the glacier that filled the upper end of the valley. This was where they needed to start using the rope and ice axes; Gertrude's long skirt, which might easily tangle in the gear, would be a nuisance and possibly a danger. Ever practical, she took it off and continued the climb in her long silk bloomers, feeling "very indecent."18

Crossing the glacier took an hour, then they rested for ten minutes on La Promontoire, a long rocky spur that juts from the south side of the ridge. Then they climbed on, spending three hours working their way up a long chimney – a wide groove in the rock – followed by some easy slopes. Gertrude was impressed at how well she'd done so far as they rested again; this was easy, she thought. She was about to get an unwelcome surprise – now came the most difficult part of the ascent. In fact it was more than difficult; it was terrifying. Twice she had to be hauled up on the rope where the handholds were too far apart for her to reach. Worse was going round corners on the almost vertical precipice, where there was no-one above to hold a rope. Within minutes of leaving the second rest stop she was convinced she was going to die; she knew she was far too inexperienced to be up here. With her usual determination she kept going, though, and "presently it began to seem quite natural to be hanging by my eyelids over an abyss."

As the sun rose she climbed over the Pas du Chat, which she found to be no worse than the rest of that stretch, only to be told by her guides that it was the most feared place on the whole mountain. An hour and a half later, after climbing the short but steep Glacier du Carré they reached the top of the ridge 200 feet below the highest peak and for the first time Gertrude could see down into the valley on the other side of the ridge. There was La Grave far below her, almost the view of the town she'd promised herself two years before. Almost – but not quite. Having come so far she was determined to reach the summit. Just after 10 o'clock in the morning, after one last scramble up a vertical slab called the Cheval Rouge and a dangerous ascent of a 20-foot overhang, she did. Standing there in her heavy boots, jacket, thick woolen socks and dirty knee-length silk knickers, she soaked up the triumph of what she'd done.

Gertrude slept for half an hour on the highest peak of La Meije then, with Turner (who was completely exhausted and looking ill) and her guides, she started down again. This time they dropped off the ridge to the northeast, descending a series of small cliffs with the ropes then angling down to the top of the Glacier du Tabuchet. This glacier now draws crowds of extreme skiers; then it was the upper limit of where less dedicated mountaineers might reach, so Gertrude unpacked her skirt and made herself decent. The glacier was treacherous and infested with dangerous crevasses, so the rope was in use until they came off its base onto the long green alpine meadow that sloped down to La Grave. She revived Turner by feeding him chocolate and water then, chatting happily to the young man, walked down into the town. Reaching her hotel around 6:30 pm she was surprised to receive a hero's welcome; most of the guests had been waiting for her on the doorstep and the owner let off firecrackers in her honor. By the time the two Germans – Dr. Paulke and Lieutenant Lohmseller – arrived a couple of hours later she was bathed, changed and enjoying an enormous dinner, after which she went to bed.

Next morning she sent her father a telegram to let him know she was safe, then sat down to write him a long letter about the climb. She felt "a wicked satisfaction," she wrote, before going on to say she had almost no money left to pay for the journey home and planned to write some large checks on his account.

Sir Hugh must have been relieved that his daughter had survived her mad adventure, but if he hoped it had gotten the urge to climb out of her system, he was about to be disappointed. Her letter proudly announced that Lieutenant Lohmseller had written to the Deutschen und Österreichischen Alpenverein – the German and Austrian Alpine Club – proposing her for membership. Gertrude Bell was planning on climbing a lot more mountains.

CHAPTER 6: ONWARDS AND UPWARDS

In fact Gertrude was so eager to continue mountaineering that instead of returning home right away she started planning another expedition. The highest peak in the southern half of the French Alps, the Barre des Écrins, was only six miles to the south of La Meije and a determined climber could reach it from the Refuge du Carrelet, another mountain hut, in a day. Her guides agreed, but insisted that she spend another day or two on practice climbs first. They scrambled around the rocky valleys near La Grave, finding the most difficult climbs they could and scaling them repeatedly. The practice was essential, the guides told her; the Barre des Écrins was dangerous. The north face of the mountain was mostly covered in glacial ice, which Gertrude wasn't so confident on, and the rock of the south face was crumbling and treacherous. So she practiced, and in between practice climbs she shopped. She was short of cash by the standards of the Bell family, although most people wouldn't have thought she was all that hard up – she had about £25 left, equivalent to around $3,500 in 2014 dollars. By the time she settled her hotel bills that wouldn't be enough to get her home to Yorkshire, but she did manage to buy a pair of men's pants to wear under her skirt when climbing. When the going got hard she could take the skirt off without exhibiting her underwear, which wasn't actually any more revealing than the pants but would cause some comment if polite society got to hear about it. Of course well-bred ladies wouldn't wear pants in public either, which was why she kept her ankle-length skirt on until she started the tough ascents.

By August 30, Gertrude had managed to persuade the guides she was ready to attempt des Écrins. They probably weren't convinced, but they'd learned by now that when the slim Englishwoman with the flaming red hair had made her mind up, it was best to just agree. That afternoon they left La Grave and walked round the towering mountains to the refuge. There they met Monsieur Faure, a French climber Gertrude had already encountered who, as well as his son had a surprising friend with him. It was Prince Luís of Órleans-Braganza, who had been exiled in 1889 when Brazil became a republic and was now in the Austrian army. Gertrude, comfortable as ever chatting to royalty, found him "a nice little boy" (the prince was 21 but looked "absurdly young").19 Perhaps she had some influence on him, because when the First World War began 15 years later Luís changed sides and became an officer in the British Army. For now she shared his soup. As they were eating, her two German friends, Paulke and Lohmseller, arrived. It would have been crowded in the refuge that night. These mountain huts were a blessing to climbers; they acted as bases expeditions could be launched from, and a safe shelter in bad weather. For Gertrude they also offered liberation. Far from her privileged world of chaperones and class divides, here was a place where the mostly aristocratic mountaineers mixed freely with guides and servants; and men and women slept, wrapped in travelling cloaks, on the same straw-covered platform. The comforts of the huts were spartan; the Refuge du Carrelet had a single saucepan that each party used in turn. The Germans had their own equipment and cooked "an excellent dinner" outside the hut. Then the group sat around watching the sunset, planning the next day's climb, until they turned in for an early night. Just after midnight they were up again, and after mugs of hot chocolate they set off. By dawn they were high on the mountain, looking down on a sunlit sea of white cloud.

It was bitterly cold on des Écrins. High winds moaned constantly round the upper slopes, chilled by the glaciers they swept over on the way. So far they had been working their way up steep but easy slopes; the difficult part of the climb lay ahead. After a break for lemonade it was "skirts off and straight up the rock." Now Gertrude's education about the hardships and hazards of mountaineering really began. The cold stiffened ropes and numbed hands; Gertrude sat on hers to keep them warm while they waited for a lost ice ax to be retrieved. Then, as they worked their way across a glacier, she had her first real climbing accident. As she settled her boot on a rock it sheared away under her and she sprawled on the ice. One of her guides, Mathon, caught her on the rope but a sharp rock he was holding broke as he took her weight and the splinters cut his hand badly. Now it was "Germany to the rescue, as usual."20 She had already been impressed by the packets of powdered lemonade mix the Germans carried with them; now Dr. Paulke produced a first aid kit and bandaged Mathon's hand. He also had one of the new sticking plasters for Gertrude's finger, which she had cut on the ice.

The rock didn't get any safer as they climbed. Prince Luís and his group were slightly ahead of them and their progress was sending down showers of broken rock, which forced Gertrude's party to wait until the prince had finished each stretch before they could safely follow. Waiting was miserable as the cold wind sapped their strength, and when they could move again they had to pace themselves carefully. Over-exertion would have led to sweating, which would have been extremely dangerous when they stopped again. It was ten o'clock when they finally hauled themselves up the last stretch to the summit and stood there, looking through the clear air at the Alps spread out before them. Among the summits was the Matterhorn; Gertrude marked it out as a future goal. They stayed on the peak for an hour and a quarter, taking photographs. Gertrude took the chance to sleep for twenty minutes. Then they crossed over the summit to the ice-covered northeast slope and started down the glacier.

The Glacier Blanc curves down from the summit, turning east and finally southeast, for a distance of over three miles. At one stage, the two Germans had to spend an hour roping down an almost sheer wall of ice, cutting steps in the packed snow that covered it so the others could follow. By the time Gertrude got to the bottom, three fingers on her left hand were

badly frostbitten from gripping the steps. It
took nearly five hours to descend the glacier,
and Gertrude – who wrote "I'm a dreadful duf-
fer at ice" (but went on to say "but rather good
at rock by this time") - fell twice. By the time
she reached the bottom she was limping from
the pain of a twisted ankle and her new pants
were hanging in ribbons around her legs. Her
fingers were so frozen she couldn't even fasten
her skirt; Mathon had to button it for her. Then
they turned north towards La Grave. At 8pm
they reached the inn to find that the owner,
warned of their approach, had a huge dinner
ready.

Gertrude had managed another formidable
peak. She wasn't the first woman to climb des
Écrins but was probably the first to go up the
more dangerous southern side. It had been a
struggle though; her ankle was hurting her and
her frostbitten fingers were badly blistered. In
a letter to her father, she complained that 19
hours of almost constant climbing was too
much, and that, after all that, des Écrins had
been less interesting than La Meije. A less determined individual might have given up on

mountaineering at that point. Not Gertrude. On Saturday, September 2, she moved from La Grave to the tiny village of Ailefroide, twelve miles to the south, and that night was spent in another mountain hut with her guides and the Germans. On Sunday, she climbed the 12,946-foot Mont Pelvoux. That, she declared, was one of the nicest days she'd had.

Another side to the Bell family emerges here in Gertrude's letters to her father. She mentions a poor local family to whom Sir Hugh had apparently given 100 Francs on their family holiday in the region, and passed on a message that another 200 Francs would let the family's son study as a priest. That an outspoken atheist would recommend her father finance this ambition shows a deep generosity hidden behind her often spiky exterior.

CHAPTER 7: SWITZERLAND

The Alps just sneak into a list of the world's twenty longest mountain ranges, taking 19th place. That's deceptive, though; they're a lot more extensive than their 750 mile length suggests. The Andes, the longest range in the world, runs in a more or less straight line down the western side of South America; the Rockies, in second place, do pretty much the same in the western USA. The Alps form a wide, sprawling crescent that curves north from the southern coast of France into Switzerland, swings east through northern Italy and Monaco, takes in parts of Germany and most of Liechtenstein and finally straggles out in Austria and Slovenia. There are about 340 mountains in the range with Mont Blanc, at 15,781 feet, being the highest. Five of them, including the notorious Matterhorn, are higher than anything in the Rockies and 82 peaks (not all of them classed as separate mountains) reach over 13,000 feet. By the time winter started to close in around the summits in late 1899 Gertrude had climbed several of the toughest peaks in the French part of the range. She returned to Yorkshire as an experienced mountaineer and was already planning more ambitious expeditions for the next year.

Mont Blanc, she said, had been mocking her across Lake Geneva. That was typical of Gertrude's understatements. Mont Blanc wasn't mocking her; it was threatening her with real danger. The massive peak is technically less difficult than some stretches she'd already climbed but its size and the freezing environment near the summit make it a killer. Even with today's far superior climbing equipment and outdoor clothing about a hundred mountaineers die every year on the Mont Blanc massif. By the time Gertrude reached Chamonix on August 1, 1900 and met her new guides, the unfortunately named Führer brothers, the mountain had already claimed over a thousand lives. The weather was foul, too; even in August, fresh snow was falling and while that didn't worry her much – she planned to stick to rock for most of the route and avoid the glaciers, where snow was most dangerous – there were also high winds around the summit.21

Gertrude had made the mistake of sending her heavy baggage by a separate train, and it got delayed on its way to Chamonix, so for a few days she sat in her hotel with Ulrich and Heinrich Führer and worked on her maps. When the trunks with her climbing gear finally arrived, she was ready with an ambitious program of climbs while she waited for a chance at Mont Blanc. She had now equipped herself with a man's climbing suit tailored to fit, although she still wore a skirt over it on the lower slopes. As soon as the climb became difficult enough to need hands the skirt would be removed and her trim figure, smartly turned out in blue breeches, tunic, men's shirt and even a necktie, soon became a familiar sight on the Swiss alpine summits. Other female climbers began dressing in the same style, following the example of the increasingly famous redhead. This might only be her second climbing season, but Gertrude was already becoming a personality on the mountains; the diaries of other mountaineers mention her frequently.

Twice in mid-August she climbed the lower slopes of Mont Blanc, only for her guides to insist on turning back as the weather worsened. Finally, on August 20, they decided the weather was just good enough for them to press on and, accompanied by a young Englishman named Urquhart, they scrambled the final 3,000 feet to the summit. They had made the usual early start, leaving the mountain hut long before dawn, so they were in time to stop for breakfast at the Vallot Observatory not far from the summit. After eating, they continued through deteriorating weather to the top, and barely reached it when mist and swirling snow closed in around them. Gertrude photographed the Janssen Observatory, a tiny hut perched right on top of the mountain, but there wasn't much time. They quickly headed back to the Vallot building for a second breakfast.

Not long afterward, however, the snow became heavier, and one of the guides warned that they had to get moving. The weather was already bad and getting rapidly worse; the air was heavy with static electricity, sending sparks from the tips of ice axes that were intense enough to singe one man's beard. The scientists told them that to avoid the approaching storm they had to be well below the summit inside an hour, so they raced down toward the relative safety of the lower slopes. They seem to have gone too fast for safety but they were a skilled, confident group – and a daredevil one. At one point Gertrude, Ulrich Führer and Urquhart lost their footing and slid down a glacier; if another guide, Schwartzen, hadn't already made it across that stretch and anchored the rope they would probably have joined the long list of Mont Blanc's victims. Gertrude was "lying spread eagle wise, quite helpless with ice and laughter."22 She was intelligent enough to know the danger of what she was doing, but for her it was all part of the fun. As they descended they met another group on their way up, and warned them they should turn back. The climbers refused and struggled on towards the summit; they ended up trapped in the Janssen Observatory for two days while a blizzard raged around them. Gertrude reached her hotel in time for a late lunch, "pleased and dirty." Unfortunately the storm put an end to any more mountaineering for the next two days, and in one of her long letters she complained to her father that she hated hanging around when she could be climbing.

These weather-enforced delays were a real irritant to Gertrude. She teased Sir Hugh in letters about how he would react when he saw the bills for her expeditions, but there were limits to her budget and she couldn't keep guides around indefinitely. When the blizzard blew itself out on Wednesday, 22 August, her contract with the Führers had only two more days to run. Determined to make the most of it she raced up two more peaks in the Mont Blanc Range, the Aiguille du Grépon and the Aiguille du Dru. "Aiguille" is French for "needle" and it's appropriate - both mountains are towering, slender pinnacles of dangerous rock.

On August 20, 1901 she was back in Switzerland, with the Führers booked for another month of climbing. After spending that night in Basel her destination on the 21st was the town of Meiringen in the Bernese Alps – one of the highest and most challenging sections of the range. Her confidence in her own abilities had reached new highs after the successes of 1900, and she was eager to try even harder peaks. To get back in shape, she stayed in Meiringen about as long as it took her to change into her climbing outfit and send a quick telegram home, and then set out that afternoon for a mountain hut. On August 22, she breezily climbed the 12,113-foot Wetterhorn on the way to her new base in Grindelwald. On the 23rd she and the Führers climbed to the Schwartzegg hut ready for an attempt at the forbidding Schreckhorn the next day. Like many of the huts, this one was far above the tree line so as they climbed they gathered bundles of firewood and carried them up the mountain. In the evening they relaxed around the hut – Gertrude met a friendly groundhog – then went to bed for another early start. By seven the next morning, they were on top of the Schreckhorn. Returning to the hut they found two young Frenchmen burning their firewood and drinking their tea. Gertrude told them with icy politeness that she was pleased to entertain them but hoped they would let her have some tea. When she returned from putting her skirt on she found they had fled, leaving a note in the visitor's book: "We climbed to the refuge without guides. Splendid view but very hungry. Fortunately we found some tea." The note was in French, of course, but Gertrude spoke the language fluently. She added a neat explanation – "N.B. It was my tea!" - and signed it.23

Drinking their liberated tea outside the hut, Gertrude told Ulrich Führer about her latest plan. The highest mountain in the Bernese Alps is the Finsteraarhorn, a lethal spike that rises to 14,022 feet. Only a handful of climbers had ever reached the summit and none had ever succeeded in climbing the north-east arête, a knife-edged ridge rising steeply to the peak. Only three expeditions had tried, and all had been forced to turn back. Gertrude was determined to give it a go. Ulrich reluctantly accepted the challenge, but worried that she was becoming dangerously overconfident.

Before attempting the Finsteraarhorn they set out to tackle the Engelhörner ridge. Much of it had been climbed before but Gertrude wanted to be the first mountaineer to do them all one after another. Fresh snow kept them out of the high peaks for a few days so she occupied herself training with Ulrich in the valleys, then on the 29th headed for the ridge. Heinrich Führer had been drafted into the Swiss Army and left them on August 31, and was replaced as a guide by his cousin, also (confusingly) named Heinrich Führer. Together they climbed the peaks along the ridge, one by one, in one of the most impressive feats of sustained mountaineering ever. They were breaking new ground now. Two of their ascents were along never-used routes. Seven took them to previously unclimbed summits. It was a triumph, and it pushed her confidence higher than ever. On September 7, as Ulrich had worried, she finally went too far.

The Grosses Engelhorn is one of the highest points of the ridge. At only 9,127 feet it was a pygmy compared to some of the mountains Gertrude had already scaled, but it was truly dangerous and the worst route to the summit was along the ridge. Nobody had ever managed to reach it along the exposed traverse and Gertrude was determined to be the first. It was a frightening prospect. Deep snow, dizzying angles and disintegrating rock made a formidable series of obstacles and traps. Where the limestone wasn't crumbling it had been polished to a glassy smoothness by ice and water.

On Friday, September 6, the trio climbed high into the Ochscuthal, a valley perched on the upper slopes of the ridge, then began working their way along the jagged crest. They ran into blowing snow, which forced them back down, but next day they tried again. The weather was better but the rock turned out to be even worse than they had expected, and as they fought their way higher, the guides were appalled. They finally came to an overhang too high for any of them to reach the top. Ulrich climbed on Heinrich's shoulders but couldn't grip the edge of the rock above him. Only when Gertrude stood on Heinrich's shoulders, and Ulrich perched on hers, could he make the rope fast so they could climb on – and then only when she stood on tiptoe to gain an extra inch. But Heinrich had had enough. His nerve had gone, Gertrude wrote later, and they left him tied to the rock.24 She and Ulrich raced up the towering slabs towards the summit, only to be blocked by a smooth sheet of rock too high for the two of them to get up. Frustrated, they dropped down a few yards, then moved round to the other side of the peak and tried a new route. Gertrude finally wedged herself into a rock chimney while Ulrich used her body as a step then hauled her up the rest of the way. They emerged onto the crest only a few steps from the summit and the Grosses Engelhorn was done.

By the time they'd lowered themselves on their remaining rope and rescued Heinrich it was too late to get safely down into the valley that night, so instead of returning to the inn at Grindelwald they headed for a shepherds' hut

Ulrich knew. A wooden wall split the little building into two rooms. In one sat three shepherds,
smoking their pipes. In the other were some
enormous pigs. The shepherds, hearing where
they had come from, gave them hot bread and
milk. Then Gertrude climbed into the hay loft
and fell asleep, until the pigs woke her next
morning.

Heinrich might have lost his nerve, but Ulrich Führer seems to have been impressed at
her skill and determination (although perhaps
not her almost insane courage). The last stretch
to the summit of the Grosses Engelhorn had
been enough to frighten an experienced mountain guide to the point where he would go no
further; Gertrude wrote "I don't think I have
ever had two more delightful alpine days."
Now, as Heinrich plodded down the valley on
his own, Ulrich paid her a great compliment. He
told her that his home was close by, and took
her to a neat mountain chalet to meet his father. Swiss mountain guides would happily risk
their lives for their wealthy clients, but they
very rarely brought them home for lunch.

In many ways, 1901 was the high point of Gertrude's brief climbing career. She finished the season undefeated, and had ascended several peaks that had never been reached before. One of them was named in her honor – the Gertrudspitze, along the Engelhorn. Appropriately, the next summit is the Ulrichspitze. But she hadn't climbed the Finsteraarhorn.

In 1902, she set out to fix that. With the Führer brothers, she tackled several more climbs, just for practice – although one of them was a traverse on the Schreckhorn that everyone agreed was impossible. As it turned out, it wasn't – just nearly impossible. Then before dawn on July 31, they started the ascent of the Finsteraarhorn.

Right from the start, it was a brutal ascent. Gertrude knocked loose a piece of rock that knocked her flat on her back and sent her skidding down a sheet of ice. She managed to stop herself before coming to the end of the rope, then turned pale when, climbing to her feet, she saw that the rope had been sliced halfway through. They struggled on, cutting steps across sheets of ice and wriggling up steep

chimneys. Often they had to form a human lad-
der to get someone to the top of a vertical
rock slab, one of the dreaded "gendarmes." By
ten o'clock, the time they were usually at the
summit and thinking about racing downhill for
lunch at the hut, they were eating a cold snack
on the knife edge of rock that led to the summit. The peak of the Finsteraarhorn was in sight
now, but Gertrude could also see black clouds
sweeping in. By mid-afternoon they were
within 300 feet of the summit but blocked by a
gendarme they couldn't climb, and it was beginning to snow heavily. They scouted to the
sides of the ridge, looking for a way round, and
started along a dangerous icy path to the left.
Their hope was that they could cover the last
short stretch to the peak before turning back
for safety, but fresh snow started cascading
down across their route in a mini avalanche.
For the first time Gertrude realized she had to
turn back – but she had left it too late.

Around 8pm the first thunder cracked over
the summit. The air was thick with electricity
and blue sparks were leaping between the
rocks. They had managed to drop down from

the ridge, where the danger of lightning was highest, but feeling the steel head of her ice ax Gertrude realized that even through her glove it was warm to the touch. They scraped a hole in the loose shale and buried the axes, then looked for shelter. They found a steep crack in the rock and wedged themselves into it. Ulrich sat on Gertrude's feet to keep them warm and he and Heinrich covered their own feet with their backpacks. They roped themselves together and anchored the rope, fearing that one of them would be struck by lightning and fall from the chimney. All night they huddled in the narrow crack, trying to sleep but constantly woken by the thunder. Even in this terrifying predicament Gertrude enjoyed the power of the storm.

Slowly the storm passed and the moon came out. In the morning, the three emerged from their crack and ate a cold breakfast, livened up by a spoonful of brandy for each. Then, faced with thick mist and a rising wind that pelted them with snow, they started down again. The wind rose to a howl and the temperature rose with it, drenching them with streams of icy water as the snow melted above them. Streams of slush slithered down the mountain and the risk of avalanches was high. When they reached the glaciers on the lower slopes night was falling again; they spent it huddled on sacks above the hazardous wall of ice at the glacier's base. By the time they staggered into Meiringen next day, almost dead from exposure, they had been gone for nearly two and a half days and the entire village was buzzing with anxiety.

Gertrude, Ulrich and Heinrich were all in a terrible state. They were frostbitten, exhausted and on the edge of hypothermia. It took two days for them to recover, then there was a difficult lunch with the Führer family – her guides' mother was almost hysterical over what they'd done.25 Ulrich was more impressed. As Gertrude wrote to her father to tell him that Chirol's prediction of her dying in the Alps had almost come true the guide was writing his own letter. The climb had only been attempted three times, he told Sir Hugh, including their own failed attempt. He credited Gertrude's bravery and determination with getting them all down safely.26

For the 1903 climbing season, Gertrude was on another round the world tour, but she interrupted it to do some climbing in the Rockies. Then in 1904 she returned to Switzerland and the Führer brothers. There was one last peak she had to climb: the Matterhorn. A ragged pyramid rising to 14,692 feet, it has claimed more lives than any other mountain in the Alps. It was first climbed in 1865 by a party of seven mountaineers, four of whom died on the way back down.

As before they set out long before dawn; the sun came up on a threatening day, but soon afterwards the weather cleared and most of the climb was easy. A final stretch below the summit slowed them; it took two hours to climb 20 feet. Heinrich found it a struggle, but at ten in the morning they reached the peak of the most famous Alp of all.

And, with the Matterhorn conquered, she at last seemed content. After that she made no more great climbing expeditions, only casually climbing whatever peaks she happened to find herself near. Mountaineering had been a brief phase for her. But most people who have a sudden impulse to take up mountaineering might buy a few guide books and a pair of boots, and even enroll in a rope course at the local sport center, Gertrude had made a name for herself at the highest levels of the sport in only five seasons. As usual, when she decided to do something, she did it in style.

CHAPTER 8: A SHORT VERSION OF A LONG STORY

Even as she amazed seasoned climbers and terrified her family, Gertrude had maintained her interest in the Middle East. Her seasons in the Alps had lasted little over a month, leaving her plenty of time for other interests. She was an enthusiastic photographer and organized slide shows for the wives of Sir Hugh's workers, amazing them with photos of her climbing adventures. She spent time in London, mostly for social events or to join various societies. Travel always appealed to her, however, and when an old friend wrote to her in November 1899 and invited her to Jerusalem, she eagerly accepted.

Jerusalem is one of the world's most historic cities. Founded up to 5,000 years ago during the Bronze Age, by the Canaanite peoples, it became the capital of an Egyptian client state, then the center of a loose confederation dominated by the Israelites. In the 8th century BC, it was conquered by the Assyrians, then in the 6th century BC, the expanding Babylonian empire took control. When the Persian king Cyrus the Great added Babylon to the Achaemenid Empire, he invited the Jews of Babylon to return to Jerusalem and rebuild the (possibly legendary) Temple there. The construction of the Temple, their existing Israelite religion and the beliefs they had picked up during the Babylonian captivity fused during this period to create the modern Jewish religion. For centuries, Judea was a largely self-governing Persian client state and Jerusalem was its capital. In the late 4th century BC, the Persian Empire, the most powerful and civilized of its time, fell to the Macedonians under Alexander the Great, and Jerusalem came under Macedonian influence. Greeks began to settle there, bringing the modern Hellenistic culture that was spreading through the Mediterranean region. The Seleucids, a Hellenized empire centered in Persia, took the region in 198 BC. In 168 BC a Jewish rebel army, the Maccabees, revolted against the Greek culture of their rulers and established a theocracy, the Hasmodean Kingdom of Judea, forcing the large Greek population to convert to Judaism and imposing religious law. Then, around 67 BC, a civil war broke out between the rival Pharisee and Sadducee factions of the priesthood; the Sadducees believed that the Torah was the sole legitimate source of religious law, while the more moderate Pharisees preferred the oral law. This was uniquely bad timing for a disruptive squabble, because their new neighbors were already annoyed.

For the last century the Roman Republic, following its annihilation of Carthage during the Third Punic War, had been steadily expanding its influence through North Africa and the Middle East. Often the expansion was reluctant; Rome, trying to pacify new territory, would find its efforts being disrupted by refugees or armed groups thrown up by conflicts beyond its borders. The only way to solve the problem would be to send a few legions to end the dispute – and suddenly Rome had more land to

pacify, with new borders and new problems beyond them. By 63 BC, the Republic controlled
Ptolemaic Egypt and most of Syria, and was
fighting an intermittent war against the disintegrating Seleucid state. The trouble in Judea
was attracting raids by the Seleucids and the
Parthians, and that meant problems in Egypt.
The Hasmodean Kingdom was officially a valued ally of the faraway city on the Tiber, and
both factions sent envoys to the Roman commander in Syria, Gnaeus Pompeius Magnus –
Pompey the Great. They each hoped they
could gain Rome's support in the internal feud.

Pompey's title came from the fact that he
was a great soldier, though nobody ever called
him a great diplomat. To him, the conflict of
Pharisees and Sadducees was a pointless argu-
ment between two sides that, as far as he was
concerned, were equally wrong. He quickly lost
patience and led his legions into Judea,
stormed Jerusalem and put a Roman puppet
king, Antipater, on the throne. In 36 BC Antipater was succeeded by his son, the infamous
Herod the Great. Herod died in 4 BC and the
kingdom was divided among his three sons. In

6 AD the region was brought under direct Imperial rule as the province of Iudaea. Too small to have its own governor, it was made a satellite of Syria under the new governor Quirinius (the Cyrenius mentioned in the New Testament). Quirinius immediately upset many of the inhabitants by holding the first census of the area, which was against Jewish law. That led to decades of turmoil as the Romans, trying to find a form of government that would keep the excitable locals happy, switched between direct rule and a series of puppet kings. In 66 AD a Jewish mob, upset because Greeks were allowed to follow their pagan religious rituals, started attacking Greek merchants. When the trouble spread and Roman tax collectors began to be attacked, the Procurator of Jerusalem sent troops to the Temple to collect the taxes from the priests' treasury. The province erupted into open rebellion and the garrison of Jerusalem were captured and massacred. A hasty relief force was sent from Syria but that, too, was attacked and massacred by the rebels, leaving 6,000 Roman soldiers dead.

Emperor Nero was less than amused and in 68 AD he sent his favorite general, the out-standing Vespasian, to put down the rebellion. Vespasian's son Titus had already assembled an army in Alexandria consisting of over 40,000 soldiers from local client kings, with a Roman legion at its head. Vespasian brought two more legions, the elite V Macedonia and X Fretensis. Instead of rushing into a possible trap he methodically worked his way through the province from north to south, crushing the rebellion as he went. Jerusalem was surrounded and left for last. Obligingly, two rebel factions inside the city kept fighting each other for control and didn't join forces until the legionaries were actually building ramps up to the city walls. Then, in a crazed attempt to encourage the defenders to fight harder, their leaders burned most of the food supply. Titus finally put an end to the madness in May of 70 AD, by smashing through Jerusalem's three walls one after another and burning down most of the city. As a punishment for the massacre of the captured Roman garrison four years earlier, the few surviving inhabitants – up to a million rebels from all over the province had fled to the city, and most of them had died of starvation or disease – were sold as slaves. The Temple was left burned out and shattered by Roman siege weapons. As the city was rebuilt most of its battered remains were pillaged for stone, until only the famous Western Wall survived.

The trouble wasn't over. In 132 AD, the Bar Kokhba revolt once again overthrew the province's government. The rebels besieged the garrison in Jerusalem; smaller garrisons and many Christians were massacred. Simon Bar Kokhba declared himself Prince of Israel. Emperor Hadrian, who had invested a fortune in rebuilding Jerusalem and the province, had had enough. Bar Kokhba had a force of up to 400,000 rebels; Hadrian threw in twelve legions, each of around 5,000 Roman regulars and about the same number of auxiliary cavalry and archers. Outnumbered three to one by the rebels they faced a hard fight. XXII Deiotariana suffered so many casualties it was broken up and the survivors used to reinforce other units. IX Hispana, the famous Ninth Legion that some believe vanished in Scotland (and which reappears in many fantasy novels and bad movies) may have suffered the same fate. For three years, the legionaries grimly stormed fortified towns and hunted down rebel forces, ending in a climactic slaughter when they broke into the final fortress at Betar. Half a million rebels were killed in all; uncounted numbers of people died of plague and famine as the collapsing rebellion tore the society apart. Then Hadrian set out to finish the job.

In the space of two generations Jewish rebellions had destroyed three legions and wrecked the province twice, at enormous cost. Of course, the Romans could have accepted that the Jews didn't want to live under Roman rule and withdrawn from the region, but they weren't always very forgiving. Hadrian set out to destroy the Jewish religion and its link to Jerusalem. Every sacred object he could find was ceremonially burned on the Temple Mount, which was then decorated with statues of Hadrian and the god Jupiter. Iudaea became Syria Palastina and Jerusalem, rebuilt in the Roman style, became Aelia Capitolina. Jews and Christians were forbidden to enter the city on pain of crucifixion. The senior Jewish priests were tracked down and executed. Rome's vengeance wasn't confined to the rebels themselves as it had been after the first uprising; most of the Jewish inhabitants of the entire province were enslaved or expelled.

In fact, in trying to destroy Judaism, Hadrian made it into what it is today. By wiping out the priesthood and their link to the razed Temple he shifted the focus of Jewish religious life to the rabbis and synagogues, where it remains. The new center of scholarship moved to Babylon but scholars also studied in the communities, leading to a more decentralized and learning-focused culture in place of the often dictatorial priesthood. Jews did remain in Palastina, but in 351 AD they rebelled against Rome yet again. This time, the fault lay firmly with the Romans. By now the Empire was split into western and eastern sections and the eastern emperor in Constantinople allowed citizens to persecute the Jewish minority. Whatever caused the uprising, though, the result was the destruction of most of the Jewish communities that remained in the province. Most of the survivors converted to Christianity or the Greek and Roman pagan religions.

As the western Roman Empire fell apart in the 5th century AD, Jerusalem remained under control of the eastern empire. That control was soon challenged though, with first the Persians then an alliance of Persians and the region's surviving Jews seizing it twice. Each time the eastern empire, now known as the Byzantine Empire, managed to recapture it, the last time being in 628 AD. Then, a new conqueror out of the east swept away the last remnants of Roman rule.

Islam was founded in what is now Saudi Arabia around 610 AD, by the Prophet Mohammed. By the time he died in 632 AD, Mohammed had succeeded in unifying the tribes of the Arabian Peninsula into a single nation, which promptly found itself at war with the Byzantine Empire. A series of wars continued for over 400 years as the two empires pushed at each other, but Jerusalem fell to the Muslims early – in 634 AD – and remained in Arab hands. In the early days of Islam, the new religion's relations with Judaism were generally good, and the Caliphate removed the old ban on Jews living in the city. The Muslim rulers also signed a treaty with the Christian Patriarch to leave the holy places unmolested.

In 1099, European armies reached Jerusalem in the First Crusade and besieged the city. Most of the Christians had been expelled from the city and it was well defended, but on the night of July 14/15, siege towers were rolled up to the walls, and in the morning, the armored knights stormed across the ramparts. In the carnage that followed, the Crusaders massacred almost everyone who remained in the city.

With the Jewish and Muslim inhabitants dead or expelled, the Crusaders repopulated the city with Christians from eastern Europe and the Middle East, but in 1167 the warlord Saladin, from what is now Iraq, captured it. He expelled the "Franks" – the northern Europeans – but allowed the Eastern Christians to stay, and let Jews and Muslims back into Jerusalem. For 350 years the city was fought over by invading empires – Tartars from Persia, the Egyptian Mamluk Sultanate, and even Genghis

Khan's Mongols. By the time it finally fell to the Turks in 1517 almost every major civilization had left its mark on Jerusalem. Now, in the very last days of the 19th century, the ancient city was still part of the decaying Ottoman Empire. It had been under Turkish rule for almost four centuries, with the exception of a few years in the 1830s following a brief annexation by Egypt and the 1834 Arab Revolt. Places of worship of all three major Abrahamic religions crowded together in its streets. The neighborhoods buzzed with a chorus of languages – Greek, Judeo-Arabic, Turkish, Yiddish, even Latin. The dominant language was Arabic, though. Around 95 per cent of the inhabitants were Arabs, about one in eight of them Christians. Of the remaining 5 per cent most were Jewish, mainly recent immigrants fleeing from persecution in Russia and Poland, and a handful were merchants from Greece, Turkey, Lebanon and almost everywhere else along the shores of the Mediterranean. Into this amazing mixture of languages and cultures came the eternally curious Gertrude Bell. It was to bring about a huge change in her life. In the end it would cause even more dramatic changes for the entire Middle East.

CHAPTER 9: JERUSALEM

The capital of the Ottoman Empire was Istanbul, and that's where the embassies and senior foreign diplomats were. The Empire was huge, however, and to look after their citizens throughout it most countries had a scattering of consulates as well. Gertrude's old friend Nina Rosen was married to a German diplomat who was now the consul in Palestine. Perhaps remembering how much Gertrude had loved Persia, Nina invited her to spend the Christmas of 1899 in Jerusalem. Gertrude accepted happily; it wasn't Persia, but then she always enjoyed seeing somewhere new. To make the most of it she arranged to stay in Jerusalem for several months, packed her trunks, collected some boxes for the Rosens and set off. Stopping in London for a few days she joined the Photographic Society, went skating with millionaire travel writer and politician "Bertie" Mitford, spent some time with Sir Valentine Chirol, and then caught a boat to France. On November 29, she was in Paris and the next day she sailed from Marseilles towards Athens. A letter sent from Paris showed the cutting edge hidden behind her upper class manners:

> "Whom do you think I saw at Amiens and again at Paris? Major Forster! I fled and I don't think he saw me, but if he did, he would certainly have taken me for an unknown Russian princess, I had such a beautiful fur coat on! He was with a woman - is he married, I wonder? As I passed them I heard him say 'I'm a man who has a very small opinion of myself.' I was glad I wasn't sharing that conversation though the obvious repartee was 'Not so small as I have.'"27

On the ship to Athens, she befriended a resident of Jerusalem. He was a Syrian-born Swiss agent for Thomas Cook's travel company and "a nice intelligent civil little man," so she started interrogating him about the region she was bound for. He was happy to help her with travel advice, and even suggested some tutors who could teach her Arabic.

To say that Gertrude was good at languages would be an understatement. At this point, through school and her travels in Europe, she spoke fluent French and nearly fluent German and Persian. She could hold a conversation in Italian. She even spoke a few words of Hebrew, a language that had fallen out of use for centuries but was going through a small revival among recent immigrants from Europe.3 Now she was determined to learn Arabic too.

In Athens she did some sightseeing, visiting the ruined Acropolis and practically everything

---

3 The native Palestinian Jews spoke Judeo-Arabic (a dialect of Arabic usually written in Hebrew script), Judeo-Spanish (a colorful mix of Old Spanish, Turkish, Aramaic and Arabic that was brought to Palestine by Sephardic Jews expelled from Spain in the 15th century) or simply the local Palestinian dialect of Arabic. Immigrants from Europe spoke Yiddish and perhaps Hebrew.

else of interest in a whirlwind two-day tour, and then travelled overland to Izmir in Turkey. She had several hours free in the morning of December 7 to tour the bazaars of Izmir, pick up a few words of Turkish and have lunch with the British Consul, Henry Cumberbatch28 (whose great-grandson is the actor Benedict Cumberbatch). After lunch she found her ship for the next stage of the voyage. SS Rossiya was a small ship and Gertrude had a comfortable cabin, but the stewards spoke only Russian and the deck was crowded with 400 Russian peasants on a pilgrimage to Jerusalem. For four days they steamed through the Aegean Islands, along the southern edge of Turkey, down the Syrian coast and into Beirut. A few hours later, they set off again on the last leg of the sea voyage, to Jaffa. On December 12, the Rosens met her at the harbor and that afternoon they took the train to Jerusalem. On arrival they were met by "...a large detachment of Turkish soldiers with a band, but I think they had come more for the Komandant Pasha, who was in the train, than for us."

The German Consulate was small and all its three bedrooms were occupied; in addition to the Rosens there were their two young children and Nina's sister. Gertrude had a suite reserved at the Hotel Jerusalem, only two minutes' walk from the consulate. She had "a very nice bedroom and a tiny sitting room," which she immediately started rearranging to her own tastes. As well as photographs of her family she hung a huge map of Palestine on the wall.29 This wasn't just a social visit she was planning; she intended to explore.

Her first explorations left her with mixed feelings. "One's first impression of Jerusalem is very interesting, but certainly not pleasing," she wrote. She admired the remains of the ancient Saracen walls but "all the holy places are terribly marred by being built over with hideous churches of all the different sects." The sects fought like mad dogs, she informed her father, so that Turkish soldiers had to be posted outside every church to stop the Christians throwing stones at each other. Her cheerful impiety put an edge on her comments; "C'est le rendezvous de toutes les folies religieuses, says someone." – "It is the meeting place of all religious follies." The someone who said it was almost certainly Gertrude herself. As much as the religious conflicts in the region annoyed her, though, she quickly learned to understand and navigate them. That ability would be vital in the future when she was able to win respect from deeply religious tribal leaders.

The first thing Gertrude did once she was settled into her hotel was buy a horse, an Arab stallion. The second thing was help organize a picnic on the Mount of Olives for 50 German naval officer cadets who had arrived on a training ship (she rode to the picnic on her new horse). Then she threw herself into learning Arabic. She arranged six lessons a week, a heavy load for such a difficult language, and at first her slow progress enraged her. But slowly she began to improve. Because both languages come from a common Semitic ancestor and still have many similarities, her Hebrew got better too; she took to reading the book of Genesis in its original language.

Not all of her time was spent studying, and whenever she got the chance she was off on her new horse. Her riding was already excellent but now, as she began exploring the outskirts of Jerusalem, she started to grow frustrated at her ladies' saddle. Because women wore long, modest skirts, the usual style was for them to ride sidesaddle, which met social requirements but made it harder to control the horse and stay balanced. The uneven weight distribution was also more tiring for both horse and rider, and Gertrude was coming to hate the stiff posture it made her adopt. The Rosens suggested she try riding astride, so she borrowed Dr. Rosen's saddle and gave it a shot. It wasn't long before she bought her own men's saddle and had some nuns make her a split riding skirt. Now she could ride the way she wanted to, and the locals became used to the sight of her thundering along the roads on her galloping stallion.

Despite her lack of religion she celebrated Christmas with the Rosens; Germans do Christmas very well, and the story was woven so deeply into the history of the land around them that it was impossible not to be moved. Then, in the New Year, she set about exploring more widely. Her opinion of the Holy Land began to improve once she was out of Jerusalem itself and, with her Arabic finally becoming usable, she could talk more easily with the locals. With her new man's saddle and divided skirt, and a broad-brimmed Terai hat shielding her pale skin from the sun, she was practically dressed for exploration. There was one more interesting side effect of the new saddle she hadn't thought of before. Most men in the region wore robes or a dishdasha, so with her skirt hanging down the stallion's flanks, and her hair pinned up and mostly hidden under the hat, people assumed she was a man unless she spoke to them. In the gender-segregated society of the Middle East that was a useful thing to know.

By late February she was comfortable enough in Jerusalem that she preferred going around alone and mingling with the locals, and referred to more casual visitors as "wretched tourists."30 Now she was thinking of making some more ambitious trips out from the old city. During her short stop in Beirut she had discussed riding there through Damascus to meet the British consul, but she was developing a very strong interest in the region's history and decided that for her first big expedition she would visit the old kingdom of Moab.

The Moabites were a Semitic tribe who lived on the eastern bank of the Dead Sea during the Bronze Age. They seem to have fought frequent wars with the Israelites and at one time were a client state. Around 840 BC, they rebelled and broke free, finally becoming a client of the Assyrian Empire under Sargon II. They were later absorbed into the Persian Empire and lost their identity as a separate people, but traces of their civilization remain and Gertrude wanted to see them.

Travelling in the desert is dangerous, and it was even more dangerous in 1900. In addition to the heat, sun, lack of water and the tough terrain there was an ever-present danger from bandits or nomads. Travelling alone is madness for anyone, even those familiar with the environment, and for a wealthy European woman, it was completely out of the question. As she collected the equipment she would need for a ten-day expedition Gertrude interviewed

candidates to be her guide and cook; she finally set out on March 19 with Tarif the guide,
a cook and two muleteers to drive her pack animals. As well as an interesting trip she wanted
this to be a sort of mobile Arabic boot camp;
nobody in the small party spoke any other lan-
guage.31

The trip might not have suited the typical
late Victorian tourist, but Gertrude loved it.
She scrambled through the ruins of Persian pal-
aces and photographed the desert plants and
animals. In Madeba, she befriended the Amir
Effendi and discovered that his ambition was to
be photographed with his soldiers; she took a
photograph in exchange for one of the soldiers
to act as an escort through the desert. She
learned the routine of a camp. She also learned
the hazards of the region; several times they
met armed bandits, who were only deterred by
the rifle of their military escort. Every fact was
filed away in her active mind for future refer-
ence. They travelled 70 miles east then south
from Jerusalem, carried out the planned tour of
Moab then, tired but happy, set off on the return trip. And then, as she had often done in

the Alps, she started to give in to her wilder impulses.

The plan had been to continue south to Kerak then head west, around the southern end of the Dead Sea, and back up to Jerusalem. As they camped for the night in the shadow of Kerak's old Crusader castle, however, she struck up a conversation with an English doctor and his wife and the talk turned to the ancient city of Petra.

Set in a natural basin surrounded by cliffs of rose-pink sandstone, Petra was first inhabited around 9,000 years ago. By the time of the Romans, it had grown into a sophisticated city with a complex irrigation system, creating a natural oasis in the middle of the desert. It also sat across the main trade route from the Persian Gulf to the Mediterranean coast. The Roman scholar Pliny the Elder identified it as the capital of the Nabataeans, who grew rich on the trading caravans; to pass through, Petra travelers had to wind their way along a narrow passage, barely twenty feet wide in places, flanked on both sides by towering cliffs. There was no choice but to pay the Nabataean tolls.

112 | *Queen Of the Desert*

Later, the city picked up Greek and Egyptian influences, became part of the Roman Empire then went into decline. It was badly damaged by an earthquake in 551 AD, and finally abandoned when the Arabs took the region in 663. Now only ruins remain, including many homes carved into the soft pink rock. It lay 60 miles — three days' travel — south of Kerak. Gertrude decided that she had to see it.

Of course it wasn't as simple as just setting off. The Ottomans had overthrown the Byzantine Empire in 1453, when Constantinople was conquered and became Istanbul, but they seemed to have inherited its love of complex, entangled bureaucracy. Gertrude was in Kerak. She wanted to travel to Petra. To travel from Kerak to Petra, you needed a permit. Luckily, when she finished her tea with Dr. Johnston and returned to her own camp, she found a government official who had come to find out who she was. Knowing that the Ottomans were "desperately afraid of the English" she told the man she was German and asked for a permit to travel to Petra. Next day, March 25, she got one. She also got a new military escort to

replace the previous one, who had to return to
Madeba. Another English party, a missionary
and his wife, wanted to go with her so they
agreed to set off at dawn on the 26th.32 That
left Gertrude with the rest of the day free, and
there were small mountains around Kerak, so
she climbed one. Then her attention turned to
the Turkish army barracks. She was keen to
have a look around it but Dr. Johnston warned
that she would never get permission. She was
already learning the ways of the Middle East
though, so she didn't bother asking for permission; she just walked in the gate and cheerfully
announced that she was here to be shown
around. After her guided tour she was invited
for coffee by a group of Turkish women – her
Arabic was good enough by now to have a
lively conversation – did some more sightseeing then went shopping.

"We bought a lamb today for a medjideh
- under 4 shillings - which seems cheap.
He was a perfect love and his fate cut me
to the heart. I felt if I looked at him any
longer I should be like Byron and the

goose so I parted from him hastily - and there were delicious lamb cutlets for supper!"

Chapter 10: Queen of the Desert

By the time Gertrude returned to Jerusalem, her planned ten-day trip had stretched to 18 days and more than double the distance covered. She had learned much about travelling in the desert, including that even her Terai hat didn't give enough protection against the sun. Her face was burned a dark red by the energy reflecting up from the sand and rocks, and on future trips she wound a traditional Arab keffiyeh scarf round her head. The danger of robbery or assault by the ever-present Beni sakhr bandits was a challenge too, but that was easily solved; many travelers had problems arranging a military escort from the Turkish authorities, but Gertrude seemed to have a genius for charming local officials into lending her soldiers. Later, when that became impossible, she had the money to buy a heavy Webley service revolver and plenty of space under her petticoats to hide it.

In addition to finding solutions to practical difficulties, she was learning her way around the complexities of desert society. The Ottoman bureaucracy was elaborate and difficult to deal with except through long, flowery negotiations. The Arab tribes had their rules too; she had learned that the first thing to do on entering a camp was visit the headman. What's remarkable is how quickly she was assembling the store of knowledge, both technical and cultural, needed to survive in such a harsh environment. By any reasonable standard she was a complete novice. She'd spent less than three weeks touring in the desert, much less than many of the "wretched tourists." She wasn't a tourist any more, though. She was even learning to deal with Arab attitudes to the role of women. At five foot six inches and with red hair flowing halfway down her back she couldn't hide the fact that she was a woman, but she was discovering that if she dressed and acted similarly to a man the Arabs, maybe out of sheer confusion, could be nudged into treating her like one. As it had on the mountains of Switzerland, her confidence grew rapidly.

It must have seemed that she was becoming over-confident again in late April, when she decided to travel into the Druze country and possibly on to the Syrian coast. The Druze are a tightly knit people who follow their own distinctive religion, a blend of Shia Islam, Christianity, Gnosticism and many other branches of theology and philosophy. Mainstream Muslims think they're heretics. Even today they form a parallel culture in the countries where they live – mainly Syria, Lebanon and Israel – and in 1900 they were a closed society. No western woman had ever travelled alone among them before.

Gertrude nearly wasn't the first. Her first stop was Bosra, on the edge of the Druze country, where she had to negotiate with the local Arab chief. The mudir, appointed by the Ottomans, could grant or deny permission for her to travel on into the Druze country. She knew he was likely to deny it, so she went for the simple solution: she lied. She told the irritable official that she planned to ride to Damascus, stopping at an archaeological site first. The mudir didn't seem to believe her though, and that night she overheard him tell one of her team that she wasn't to leave Bosra without his permission. Being delayed by some petty Ottoman official wasn't part of the plan. At two the next morning, May 3, the expedition were awake and quietly packing their camp. At four, the darkest moment of the night, they slipped away from Bosra and the sleeping mudir.33

With her journey through the Druze, Gertrude really came into her own as a desert traveler. The fierce, proud warriors took to her immediately; all the way through their country she was given escorts of Druze men, invited to meals and shown every archaeological site along the way. Most of this treatment was down to the way she'd handled her first meeting with a Druze chieftain, the formidable Yahya Beg. In every village she was an honored guest – in many she found Yahya Beg's messengers had beaten her there and a reception was being prepared for the "queen".34 By the time she reached Damascus, escorted by three more soldiers donated by a Turkish commander, she was completely at home in the desert.

The desert dwellers thought so, too. On the next leg of this expedition, from Damascus to the ancient oasis city of Palmyra, she fell in with a group of Agail tribesmen taking a herd of camels to market. They were worried about losing the valuable animals to bandit attacks and invited Gertrude and her soldiers to join them. As well as giving her a chance to talk to them and pick their brains for desert knowledge, the Agail now owed her a favor.35 In the barter culture of the Middle East, that was always a good thing to know.

For the next four years, much of Gertrude's time was taken up by planning her Alpine expeditions, but she could still spare time for the Middle East. In 1902, she spent two months alone in Haifa finishing off her studies in both Arabic and Persian – four hours a day of Arabic lessons, two and a half hours a day of Persian, six days a week. She was paying from her own resources now, too. In 1901, her grandfather

had amalgamated the family business with another steel company and given large amounts
of cash to his children and grandchildren, so as
well as belonging to one of the richest families
in England she now had a considerable fortune
of her own. That removed the guilt of putting a
financial burden on her father. It also took
away his last control over her activities.

With the Matterhorn climbed and her interest in mountaineering fading, she started planning a new and ambitious series of desert
journeys. The first took place in 1905. Early in
January she travelled south from Redcar and by
the 13th she was in Beirut. Moving on to Jerusalem she recruited her team and bought sup-
plies and then set out on her greatest
adventure so far. Over the space of three
months she rode through the Jebel Druze
again, past Damascus, through Aleppo and into
Turkey. Her plan was to ride all the way to Istanbul, occasionally leaving her camp behind
and making detours on the train to visit sites of
interest, but on May 17 she got a letter from
her mother saying her father was ill. Although
the letter was dated May 1, she sold her horses

and paid her staff, then caught the train the last 300 miles to Istanbul and headed straight home.

Her journey and what she'd seen encouraged her to start a new travel book, the first of five she would write about the region. By now she was a professional-standard photographer and a mediocre but enthusiastic self-taught archaeologist, so she had plenty of material. Syria: The Desert and the Sown was written after her return home – to find Sir Hugh recovered – and published in 1907. By the time it hit the shelves she was already setting off on her next expedition. On the way through Turkey in 1905 she had met Professor William Ramsay in a hotel in Konya.36 Ramsay was an expert on Turkey and on the archaeology of the New Testament. He was also a former atheist who had become a Christian after several of his discoveries seemed to confirm the historical accuracy of the Book of Acts. Gertrude was intrigued by the idea of working with him and in 1907 they spent several months excavating around Binbirkilise. This town was a center of Byzantine Christianity in the 3rd to 8th centuries and

its modern Turkish name means "A thousand
and one churches." There aren't that many –
the ruins of around 50 have been found – but
Gertrude and Ramsay were kept busy anyway.
She arrived in Binbirkilise in mid-May, and Ramsay joined her ten days later. By the time they
finished work on July 1237 they had excavated
dozens of churches and copied thousands of in-
scriptions from all around the area. In 1909
they jointly released a book on the project, A
Thousand and One Churches, illustrated with
Gertrude's photographs. Sadly, when she returned to the site that year she found that
many of the ruins had been pillaged by locals
who had carted away tons of stone. Today, the
damage is even more extensive. It's a common
problem for archaeologists – old structures are
a good source of shaped stone for people who
might not be able to quarry it themselves – and
doesn't just affect rural areas. Many of Rome's
churches are built with blocks looted from the
Coliseum.

Being in one place for months had made it
easier for Gertrude's family to keep in touch
with her, and she made regular trips to the

British consulate in Konya to collect her mail. It wasn't long before she made friends with the military consul. A decorated veteran of the Boer War and Chinese rebellion who'd been seriously wounded twice, Major Charles Hotham Montagu "Dick" Doughty-Wylie was delighted to meet the well-known writer and explorer and invited her to lunch on her first visit. He looked forward to hearing some of her stories and besides he could do with some pleasant company; he didn't get along very well with his wife of three years. He soon found that he had no trouble getting along with Gertrude Bell, and when she returned to England the two kept up an increasingly friendly correspondence.

Her 1909 visit to Binbirkilise was part of the longest journey of her career. Starting from Aleppo in February, she had struck out east to the Euphrates River and crossed it, then followed it south to Baghdad. Along the way she investigated and photographed everything of archaeological interest she could find. Baghdad is the junction of the Euphrates and the Tigris, the two great rivers of Mesopotamia, and on reaching the city she turned north again up the Tigris. This expedition was her largest yet but when the caravan of a dozen people was plodding too slowly for her taste she would head off with one mule, a guide and a light tent.38 She followed the river right to its source, through Persia and into Turkey, finally ending in Kayseri on June 23. There she sold her hordes, paid off the team and travelled to Istanbul by car and train, stopping to look at Binbirkilise on the way.

Her letters from Kayseri and later contain the first rumblings of the approaching world war. There was unrest among the Ottoman Empire's Armenian population, with threats of a massacre of Turks followed by actual massacres of Armenians. Tension was rising between the Ottoman regime and the free states of the Balkan League; three years later the First Balkan War would erupt, wiping out the remaining Ottoman territories in Europe. Gertrude wrote that, when she got back to England, she planned to have a long conversation with David Lloyd George, a senior minister in the Liberal government, about the political situation in Turkey.39

As well as talking about briefing the Chancellor of the Exchequer – the second-most powerful man in the British government – she was also involved in other political activities around this time. The movement for women to be given the vote was gaining momentum in Britain, with the Suffragette movement drifting towards more radical tactics. Florence was opposed to women's suffrage, believing that working-class women had enough to cope with anyway and involvement in politics would simply add to their problems. Surprisingly Gertrude, despite her independence and ability to match most men at almost anything, agreed. As she was now becoming a fairly well known personality, the British Women's Anti-Suffrage League made her their honorary secretary.

Most of her attention was focused on the Middle East, however, and she could see that the situation was deteriorating slowly. She was very familiar with the inner workings of the Ottoman Empire by this time and it must have been obvious to her that it couldn't survive much longer. Now her aim was to get as much travelling done as she could before the collapse came and the region fell into anarchy. In 1911 she set out from Damascus, crossed the desert to Baghdad and finished measuring a ruined Babylonian palace she had examined in 1909. Then she swung north up the Tigris, through southern Turkey (it's possible that by this time she was as much interested in the political situation there as in the ruins) and back down to Aleppo.

In spring 1912, Gertrude was at home when Major Doughty-Wylie arrived, without his troublesome wife. The unpredictable Lily was visiting her mother in Wales and the Major, feeling that wife and mother-in-law together were more than he could cope with, had headed off to the capital in the hope of meeting his friend. When he let Gertrude know he was staying in his old apartment she suddenly decided she needed to make a major shopping expedition to London that would probably take several weeks. It turned out to be one of the high points of her life. She had many friends in London so there was always somewhere to go.

Doughty-Wylie had picked up some fresh hero-
ism in 1908 when a mob had begun slaughter-
ing Armenians near Kunya; he'd put on his
British Army uniform, taken command of a unit
of Turkish soldiers, and put a stop to the riot-
ing. He'd been shot in the arm in the process,
but not too badly, and the Ottoman government had given him another medal for bravery.
He made an interesting companion to intro-
duce to London society. Unfortunately he was
still a married companion, and Gertrude was
falling in love with him.

When Lily Wylie arrived in London a few
weeks later Gertrude quickly escaped back to
Yorkshire, uncharacteristically confused. She
could tell that Doughty-Wylie was as attracted
to her as she was to him but of course he was
inconveniently married. By the standards of the
time Gertrude was outrageous in many ways,
but there was no way she would consider an affair with a married man. That left a divorce the
only hope (although Lily might have been un-
wise to join her on a desert expedition), and to
force a decision one way or the other she invited him to her parents' home, Rounton, for a

few days in July 1913. By carefully tweaking the dates she engineered things so he would arrive without his wife.

Gertrude was 44 at this point and the only relationship of her life had been with the long-dead Henry Cadogan. She had never seemed to worry about this, but now she was convinced she had found the ideal match. They shared many interests, including a love of the Middle East, and had similar personalities. They were even within a few days of each other in age. It was just appalling luck that when she finally met him he was recently married, to the troublesome Lily. In the circumstances, it says a lot for Gertrude's character that she chose such a direct solution; she simply brought him onto her own territory and told him how she felt. Sadly, her approach may have been too direct, even for a war hero. The next day Doughty-Wylie fled back to London and Lily. Their exchange of letters continued but slowly lost its passion. It's possible he had decided to make an effort at saving his marriage. Gertrude, humiliated and rejected, threw herself back into her adventures.

Her final desert expedition began in 1913, and it was spectacular. She had planned a fairly conventional trip through Syria, but was told that the conditions were as good as they would ever be for a trip into the central highlands of the Arabian Peninsula – the fearsome Nejd. She couldn't get enough money from her own funds on such short notice so she asked her father for a loan – in a letter signed "Ever your tiresome daughter, Gertrude"40 – then planned the grand expedition. With her party mounted on camels, they set off in mid-December for a journey of over 600 miles, through some of the most inhospitable deserts on the planet, deep into the heart of what is now Saudi Arabia. On February 24, 1914 she made camp within sight of the city of Ha'il, her destination, and the next day rode into the city. She had sent two of her party ahead to announce her arrival and was welcomed as an honored guest, but this was to be one of her strangest experiences.

Ha'il was the citadel of the Al-Rashid tribe, long-time rivals to the Al-Sauds. They were more religiously tolerant than their strict

Wahhabi counterparts but they were bandits. The emir of the tribe was out raiding so Gertrude started exploring the city on her own, but then she started running into problems. She had sent a letter of credit to the emir's treasurer, but he was now away raiding with the emir and she was told she couldn't get any money until he returned – in a month. Gertrude was convinced the emir's grandmother controlled the treasury in his absence and could hand over the £200 (about $22,000 in 2014 dollars) authorized by the letter, but the old woman assured her she could not. Then the emir's deputy and his brother returned the gifts she had brought them, an ominous sign (although, as one of the gifts was a revolver, it increased her personal arsenal). Her camels disappeared and she was told they had been taken to graze on land a few miles from the city. Finally she was warned that she could not leave, or even wander around the city, without permission. By now she was sure the Al-Rashids didn't want to let her go, and with their reputation a ransom attempt was far from impossible. Long negotiations with the immensely powerful chief eunuch, Sa'id, achieved nothing; she was a virtual prisoner in a bandit stronghold deep in the desert.

On March 6 she lost her temper.

Sa'id was holding court in his tent with the leading (i.e. male) citizens of Ha'il when a small furious figure haloed by a mane of flaming red hair burst in and sat down uninvited. From Sa'id's perspective it was all downhill from there. In the Arab world, everything is discussed in a roundabout way; it's extremely rude to come straight to the point, which is why nothing can ever be done quickly there – the Arabic expression Inshallah, meaning "If God wills it," has been described as "Mañana without the urgency." Gertrude came straight to the point. In fact she came straight to several points, including her money, her camels and the fact that she would go wherever she wanted without asking permission from the Al-Rashids. Then she stood and walked out without making the usual elaborate farewells, which only the highest sheikhs were allowed to do.41 In a few minutes, she had ripped apart every social convention of the Arab world, and she had done it in an isolated fortress controlled by touchy armed bandits whose honor she had just shredded. Any experienced traveler in that part of the world would agree that what she had done was a spectacular and effective way of committing suicide.

Her camels reappeared at sunset.

Not long afterward, Sa'id the eunuch, carrying a large bag of gold sovereigns, knocked on her door and began apologizing extensively. There appeared to have been a series of most unfortunate misunderstandings which had now been cleared up, he said, and happily it turned out that her money was available after all. Naturally she also had permission to leave whenever she wanted. Just to make the point she stayed another day – she was allowed to roam freely in the town, and shown whatever she asked to see – then packed up her caravan and headed for Baghdad.

In fact, she had considered travelling even further south, but she had heard news of tribal uprisings and it was just too dangerous. The journey north was risky enough. Baghdad was 450 miles away, on the other side of an almost featureless expanse of sand, and they only stopped there for a short rest before striking out again across another 500 miles of waste-land to Damascus. By the time she arrived home in May 1914, she had truly earned the nickname Queen of the Desert.

CHAPTER 11: WAR

The Ottomans had been allies of the British Empire since the Crimean War in the mid-19th century, but alliances change, and by 1914 the crumbling Turkish-ruled superpower had transferred its allegiance to the German and Austro-Hungarian empires. That left Europe divided into two loose power blocs: the Central Powers of Turkey, Germany and Austria-Hungary on one side and the Triple Entente of the British Empire, Russia and France on the other. Thanks to accidents of geography, they had managed the impressive trick of partly surrounding each other, and both contained so many factions, mutual defense guarantees and points of tension that the whole continent of Europe was an accident waiting to happen.

On June 28, 1914, the unpopular heir to the throne of Austria-Hungary, Archduke Franz Ferdinand, was being driven through the Bosnian capital of Sarajevo when a young Bosnian Serb drew a Browning .380 semiautomatic pistol from his pocket and fired twice at the passing car. The Archduke was hit in the neck and his equally unpopular wife Duchess Sophie caught the second bullet in the abdomen. The wounded couple was rushed to the home of the governor but Sophie was dead on arrival; the Archduke died ten minutes later. It had been a straightforward political assassination: Bosnia had been annexed by Austria-Hungary six years earlier to the disgust of everyone but the Croat minority, and a mixed Serb/Muslim group had struck back. It shouldn't have had any real effect on world politics, and, in fact, it didn't even have any real effect in Austria at first; Franz Ferdinand was so unpopular that there was no public outcry and even most of the imperial family didn't bother going to his funeral. The authorities in Sarajevo didn't seem to have got the message, however. They encouraged a pogrom against the rebellious

Bosnian Serbs by the pro-Austrian Bosnian Cro-
ats (the equally rebellious Bosnian Muslims enthusiastically joined in) and several Serbs were
killed. That provoked protests from Serbia.
Austria-Hungary warned Serbia to keep out of
it. Russia told Austria-Hungary to stop threatening Serbia. Germany told Russia that if anyone was going to tell Austria-Hungary what to
do it would be Germany. By the end of July,
before anyone could really work out what was
going on, the Entente and the Central Powers
were at war.

Gertrude had returned from the desert in
late May 1914 and spent several weeks recovering in Redcar. As soon as the war broke out
she decided she was now fit and healthy, and
started to look for something to volunteer for.
She found the Red Cross, and in late November she arrived at the Wounded and Missing
Office in Boulogne, France. Her task was to col-
late casualty information into a master list for
the War Office and it was hard work, but she
tore into it at a rate that amazed her colleagues. They'd have been even more amazed
if they'd known that, after spending all day

writing lists, she spent most of the night sitting at her desk or in a local restaurant, surrounded by a blue haze of cigarette smoke and writing to Richard Doughty-Wylie. His attempt to rebuild his marriage had failed and their letters to each other were more passionate than ever.

That led to an uncomfortable meeting in December. Lily, a qualified nurse and the widow of a military doctor (her first husband had been a lieutenant in the Indian Medical Service) was posted to a field hospital nearby and invited Gertrude for lunch. Knowing that it would look suspicious to ignore the invitation she turned up, only for Lily to tell her that her husband would abandon Gertrude but never her.

Lily was wrong. Doughty-Wylie, who had been the military consul in Ethiopia, had volunteered for front line duty and was on his way home. In February 1915, he visited Lily briefly at her hospital, sympathized with her for not being able to get away from her duties then travelled on to London. From there he sent a brief telegram that Gertrude – who could get away – had been waiting for.

For three days and four nights the two of them sat in his London apartment, talking freely at last. In seven years they'd spent only a few weeks in the same country and a matter of days where they could talk privately. Their relationship had been built on increasingly passionate letters but now they could be open – and they were. She asked him to leave his wife. He replied that she had threatened to kill herself if he did. Gradually they came to an agreement that, after the war, they would be together no matter what it cost. But four nights were soon over and, reserved as Gertrude was, they still hadn't made their relationship a physical one. In an anguished letter after she'd returned to France she told him she couldn't say yes to that, so it would be easier if next time he didn't bother asking.

There wouldn't be a next time. On April 25, 1915 the British landed a strong force on the Gallipoli Peninsula 150 miles west of Istanbul. The plan was to draw German forces south from the Western Front, where the Allies were under heavy pressure, and then advance to Istanbul and cut the Central Powers in two.

Unfortunately, it was a disaster. The attackers, mostly from the Australian and New Zealand Army Corps, were pinned down on the beach by heavy artillery and machine gun fire from well dug-in Turkish defenders. One of the defenders' leaders was Mustafa Kemal, now known as Kemal Ataturk, the founder of modern Turkey. Much of his reputation came from his leadership role in the Gallipoli Campaign, the dying Ottoman Empire's last victory before the final collapse.

Doughty-Wylie, now a lieutenant-colonel, had his own leadership role to play. On the second day of the assault he led a mixed force of English and Irish infantry, whose commander had already been shot, in a furious attack to clear a village and hill whose defenders were hammering the beach. Unwilling to fire at the Turks he had lived among for years, he walked calmly ahead of his men armed only with his officer's cane. His attack swept the village clear then turned up the hill, driving the defenders down the far slope. Then, at the very moment he had achieved his aim, he was shot in the head by a Turkish sharpshooter and died instantly. For his bravery he was awarded the Victoria Cross, Britain's highest award for bravery. The medal joined his earlier award, the Order of the Medjidie for outstanding service to the Turkish state.

Lieutenant-Colonel Doughty-Wylie was buried where he fell, as were most of the casualties. After the war, the Turks moved most of the British and ANZAC bodies to a proper military cemetery at one of the landing beaches, but as a mark of extra respect, they left his on top of the hill he had captured.

Nobody wrote to tell Gertrude, and she continued to write letters until the day she was at a party and someone commented on what a pity it was he had been killed. Predictably, she was devastated. Twice in her life she had fallen in love; twice death had cheated her of happiness. She didn't fall apart though. She had written to him that she couldn't live without him but when she had to, she did. Even after the greatest blow of her life her inner strength wouldn't let her give up.

There is one curious footnote to the story of Doughty-Wylie's death. The trapped invasion force was finally forced off the beach in January 1916, leaving 53,000 dead behind. Before that, towards the end of 1915, a small figure disembarked on one of the invasion beaches. It was clearly a woman – the only one to land at Gallipoli during the whole campaign – but her face was veiled and her identity remained a secret. She didn't stay long. She just climbed to the peak of Hill 141, laid a wreath on Doughty-Wylie's grave then walked away. Historian L.A. Carlyon thought it was Lily Wylie and could be true; she was working for the French army medical service by then, and that landing beach was controlled by French forces. It isn't likely, though. As far as can be confirmed from the surviving records, Lily was working in France until long after the battered invaders evacuated from Gallipoli. But there is another possibility – another woman who had a reason to visit the grave, who often wore a veil and who had the courage and opportunity to do it.42 Gertrude Bell was back in the Middle East.

Gertrude's work for the Red Cross was important, and frantic enough to keep her mind off her personal troubles; however, it wasn't the best use of her unique talents. The Middle East was becoming an important second front in the war; much of it belonged to the Ottomans, and in January 1915 a Turkish force led by German officers raided British-controlled Egypt in an attempt to capture the Suez Canal. The British fought back, and began looking at ways to turn the Arab tribes throughout Palestine and the Arabian Peninsula against their Turkish masters. In a traditional war of front lines, trenches and mass frontal attacks, the Arab Bureau was developing a plan that would still be a masterpiece in the current age of asymmetric warfare. The Ottoman territory in the Levant and Mesopotamia – today's Israel, Jordan, Syria, Iraq and other territories – was a huge area, almost 300,000 square miles. It was crisscrossed with supply routes and railway lines that the Turks needed to supply their forces in the region, but much of it was a barren wasteland where large armies couldn't operate for long without running out of water and food. The local population was small, widely scattered and often hostile to the Ottoman authorities. The Arab Bureau knew that the resources it would cost them to spark a revolt across that vast expanse would be paid back a thousandfold by what it would cost the Turks to fight the insurgency. The trouble was, they were short of really skilled Arabists who could identify the key leaders and persuade them to rebel. T.E. Lawrence, an archaeologist and Arab linguist who'd worked in Mesopotamia before the war, had already joined the Army and been posted to Cairo. More expertise was needed though, and the Cairo Intelligence Department was having a real problem finding the right man for the job. Finally, in November 1915, they thought about asking a woman.

Gertrude sailed from Marseilles on November 21 and should have reached Port Said, Egypt, on the 25th. She was in Cairo, a hundred miles from Port Said – two hours by train, three by car – on November 30. There were ships carrying officers from Gallipoli arriving in Port Said around that time, so it's definitely possible she could have planned her journey to take her via Gallipoli. Lily Wylie is definitely known to have visited her husband's grave in

1919, after the war, but Gertrude wasn't the type to wait.

Now, in Cairo, she set about getting to know her new colleagues. The intelligence chief of the Arab Bureau was Colonel Clayton, a new acquaintance but one she liked.43 Her closest colleague was Lt Cdr Hogarth, a Royal Navy intelligence analyst with a background in archaeology, and her first job was helping him to build up area files by adding her knowledge of areas and the sheikhs who controlled them. She also found T.E. Lawrence, who she had met in 1909 while he was digging at the Hittite city of Kargamiš. In a letter to Florence she described him as "exceedingly intelligent".

Most of the work of military intelligence consists of sorting through and analyzing reports sent in from any number of sources, from spies to reconnaissance patrols to civilian refugees. Gertrude had already made herself invaluable at that within weeks of reaching Cairo. She still had more to offer, however, and Colonel Clayton knew it. In fact, her knowledge of the area was at least equal to that of Lawrence or Hogarth, partly because she was a woman.

She had treated the Arab sheikhs and emirs as her equals and largely been accepted as such, but uniquely she could also sit with the women and hear their often very different views on things. Discussions among Arab men, especially leaders, follow careful rules to ensure that nobody loses face, a failing that can lead to violence. In contrast to many western cultures, Arab women tend to give much more straightforward opinions, but a male westerner like Lawrence would never have been permitted to enter their tents or join their conversations. Gertrude had, and now it was obvious that her knowledge of the tribes, their leaders and the relations between them was unequalled. Most importantly, she had already delivered a report on the Al-Rashid tribe in the Arabian Peninsula that made clear they were so splintered by feuding, plots and assassinations that they were fast losing ground to the Al-Sauds. Clayton wanted her working on the planned Arab Revolt, but Miss Bell was a civilian and couldn't get directly involved in military operations. The colonel passed the problem up to General Maxwell, the commander of British forces in

Egypt. The message came back down from headquarters that Major Bell could get involved in anything she liked.

Gertrude hadn't gone through the Army promotion system, so the rank headquarters awarded her says a lot about how highly she was valued. In a British Army headquarters, plans are prepared at Staff Officer Grade 2 level, while Staff Officers Grade 3 do the legwork their superiors need to write the plan. Captain T.E. Lawrence, the famous Lawrence of Arabia, was an SO3. Major Gertrude Bell was suddenly an SO2. Of course, she was a rather unconventional SO2. Women couldn't officially join the British Army until the Women's Auxiliary Army Corps was formed in 1917, so there were no uniforms available for her. In a way, that was a pity; an officer's fitted tropical khakis would probably have suited her very well. As it was, she kept turning up for work in a dress and straw hat. And she had plenty of work to get done. By January 1916, she had already identified friction between the intelligence offices in Egypt and India, which was interfering with planning. The office in India was responsible for everything east of the Persian Gulf while Cairo handled everything to the west, but both had a common target: the Ottoman territories. Gertrude was already looking at the time after the war when a permanent intelligence agency would be needed to cover the region in its hoped-for post-Ottoman state, and she knew that the Indian Army's help would be vital. She was also frustrated that the intelligence office in Aden wasn't passing information to Cairo fast enough. From reading her letters it's clear that, despite her lack of military training she was a natural staff officer, with the ability to see the whole picture as well as a phenomenal mind for details.44 It was also a job she seemed to enjoy – "I am getting to feel quite at home as a staff officer! It's comic, isn't it."

She had a big problem, though. To get the Arabs to rise up against the Turks, the British had to offer them something big – bigger than gold and guns. The only bribe large enough was the promise of independence from foreign rule, underpinned by Arab nationalism. Gertrude's problem was that she knew pan-Arab nationalism was a dream. The Arabs were far too tribal to be unified. The offer of independence had to be made, but after the war was won the British government would be very reluctant to grant it. In particular, the government of India – part of the British government, but with a huge degree of independence and its own formidable army – had an eye on the Middle East as a way to expand its own territory. Gertrude was determined to do all she could to get the Arabs something approaching real independence, but first she had to help spark the revolt. Her first task was a thorough overview of the tribal structure right across the Middle East, much of it based on her own personal knowledge with the gaps filled in by material collated from other sources. Her superiors were almost in awe; it was one of the clearest, most comprehensive intelligence assessments the British Army had ever had.

Next she turned her attention to the problem of India. Yet again her gift for making friends helped out; between her old friend from Bucharest Charles Hardinge – now the 1st Baron Hardinge and the Viceroy of India – and

Sir Valentine Chirol, she managed to arrange an invitation to visit India to talk to the intelligence office there. Hardinge met her in Delhi and was quickly overwhelmed by her grasp of the situation in the Middle East. Realizing what she could achieve he suggested a new job for her: liaison between the Delhi and Cairo intelligence offices.

CHAPTER 12: BASRAH TO BAGHDAD

The liaison job was in Basrah, a port city on the Shatt al-Arab that's now in southern Iraq. The British Army has a long and not always happy history with the place. It's a miserable environment: in summer, it's a sweltering blend of desert heat, coastal humidity and filthy dust; in winter, it's a mud hole constantly drenched with lukewarm rain. In 2003 we at least had air conditioning; all Gertrude had was the frosty atmosphere of a headquarters staff that didn't want her there.

Basrah was occupied by Indian Expeditionary Force D, an Indian Army division made up of Indian and regular British units whose task was to first block any Ottoman attempt to move south along the Gulf coast, and then prepare to strike north towards Baghdad. The staff were all professional soldiers and knew their business; they had no idea why this small woman, now once again plain Miss Bell, had been sent to them. Chief political officer Major General Sir Percy Cox could have explained, but he was away from the headquarters. When he returned and explained that she had been sent personally by the Viceroy – the head of the Indian government – the staff finally showed some interest in their new member. Cox was more than a little interested himself, because he'd run into Gertrude before. In fact as British Consul General in the Persian Gulf he'd tried to prevent her 1913 expedition to Ha'il, and had been bemused to find that, once again, she had broken camp and slipped away in the night. Now he congratulated her on her achievement and decided to let her try to win over his staff.

And she did. At a working lunch in the Officer's Mess with his four senior officers, she was mercilessly grilled about the Middle East and the potential of the Arabs as allies. She answered their questions, and the generals admitted that she knew the region. She outlined the tribal structure, and they realized it was a blueprint for a guerilla army. Then she presented her master plan for a post-war Middle East, and they were hers. By the end of the day her makeshift office in a sweltering spare bedroom had been moved to a spacious, well-equipped verandah overlooking the Shatt al-Arab. Miss Bell was once again Major Bell, drawing an Indian Army salary and with two new appointments: Assistant Political Officer and Oriental Secretary.

Through 1916 and early 1917, Lawrence and others stirred up rebellion all through the Ottoman slice of the Middle East. Conventional battles between British and Indian regulars, and later newly-raised Arab armies, pinned down Turkish forces; constant raids, guerilla attacks and blown railways sapped their strength and dissipated their manpower. As the stalemate on the Western Front ground on and Russia collapsed into defeat and revolution, the tide of the war in the Middle East slowly swung in Britain's favor. Gertrude worked on, sometimes writing reports, sometimes riding into the desert to talk to sheikhs and discreetly influence them towards the new system she planned to build. When Abdul Aziz Ibn Saud visited the headquarters she was detailed to show him around and explain the British plan to him. As the leader of the extremist Wahhabi sect of Sunni Islam, Ibn Saud was appalled to be introduced to an unveiled woman who dared to treat him as an equal, but he had enough sense to realize that if he wanted continued British support for his rebellion against the Turks, he couldn't offend someone who was held in such obvious respect. Later he mocked her to his friends, including Hillary St. John Philby.

Although the British were supporting Ibn Saud, their main ally was Sherif Hussein, the leading figure in the Arab Revolt and a member of the prominent Hashemite faction, traditional rulers of the Hejaz. Ibn Saud wanted the Wahhabi sect to control the holy cities of Mecca and Medina, but both of these were in the Hejaz and under Hussein's authority. Undeterred, he had begun attacking Hussein's forces as well as fighting the Turks. Philby, a junior intelligence officer who had been trained by Gertrude, was a convert to Islam and an admirer of Ibn Saud. In 1917, he began secretly diverting support intended for Hussein to the Wahhabi leader, against the orders of Gertrude and Cox. (Treason seems to have run in the family. In 1963 Philby's son Kim, who was also an intelligence officer but had been doubled by the KGB, defected to the Soviet Union.) Philby's activities played a major part in handing control of the Arabian Peninsula to the Al-Sauds, creating Saudi Arabia, and reducing the role Gertrude had planned for the Hashemite dynasty in the post-war order.

By the beginning of 1917, it was obvious that Ottoman power in Mesopotamia was beginning to weaken. Now IEF D began planning for the advance to Baghdad, and again, Gertrude's knowledge was invaluable. She had covered much of the ground the advance would cross, so when the troops set off in February they had detailed maps of the terrain and notes on the tribes they would meet on the way. Many of those tribes, persuaded by Gertrude, were mobilized to support the advance by scouting and raiding. Baghdad fell on March 11, and two weeks later Gertrude joined Cox in the city she planned to make the capital of a new independent Iraq.

Her first priority was to start reorganizing the city's administration to get it ready for independence; her second was to find somewhere decent to stay. She had been allocated a house that turned out to be a hovel; it had no furniture or plumbing, and was located in a noisy bazaar. Rather than ask the billeting officer to find her something better she simply set off to walk around the city, and soon found a large garden with three old summer houses in it. She made some enquiries and found it belonged to a friend of hers, Musa Chalabi (the grandfather of Iraq's post-Saddam interim ruler, Ahmed Chalabi). Belonging to one of Britain's richest families had its advantages; she immediately rented the garden from Chalabi and had the summer houses renovated.45 With a modern bathroom and kitchen installed, and a staff hired to clean the little houses and put the overgrown garden back in order, it made an unconventional but beautiful home and she was delighted with it. When she invited staff colleagues there for drinks they got the strong impression that she didn't see it as a temporary residence.

With Lawrence waging an increasingly ferocious war in the Hejaz and the Anglo-Indian forces driving north from Baghdad towards Mosul and the Turkish border beyond, it was obvious that the days of Ottoman rule in the Middle East were numbered. Perversely, that made Gertrude busier than ever. A stream of emirs and sheikhs visited the headquarters, desperate for assurances that the Turks wouldn't return and that the British and French would honor their promises of independence. They were told to speak to Cox; they wanted to speak to Gertrude. Some of them called her the Mother of the Faithful, which was an incredible honor; the title was the one given to the Prophet Mohammed's favorite wife, Aisha. Others called her the Queen of the Desert.

She was determined to repay the trust they placed in her, and she used all of her knowledge and influence to steer the direction of the British occupation. Mesopotamia had to be rebuilt from the ground up before anyone could even think of independence. Fundamentals had to be changed. For five hundred years, the language of law and politics had been Turkish; now it all had to be changed to Arabic. The corrupt Ottoman system of land ownership had to be swept away and replaced. Laws had to be rewritten. Gertrude was at the heart of everything. Even if her relations with her staff colleagues were sometimes difficult, the British government recognized what she was doing. In October 1917, she was made a Commander of the Order of the British Empire. She was not impressed.

Slowly Mesopotamia stabilized. The new legal system began to operate, chaotically at first then more smoothly. In November 1918, the war ended with the armistice agreement, although the last pockets of Turkish forces held out well into 1919. With the Ottoman Empire in ruins it was time to decide what happened next, and Gertrude was ready with another of her trademark briefing papers. This one was titled Self-Determination in the Middle East.

Self-determination wasn't a popular concept in the Baghdad headquarters, though. Sir Percy Cox had been replaced by his deputy, Lieutenant-Colonel A.T. Wilson. Unlike Cox, Wilson believed that the Middle East had to be taken over by the victorious allied powers, meaning Britain and France. Gertrude violently disagreed, but Wilson was her superior and now he tried to freeze her out of the decision-making process. Wilson was a plodding military bureaucrat, and normally Gertrude would have run rings around him, but right now her energy was at a low point. She was in her early fifties now; she was suffering from serious bouts of malaria, and on top of that the heat, the poor diet of tinned food and thirty years of chain-smoking were starting to take their toll.

She did have two powerful allies. US President Woodrow Wilson and British war minister Winston Churchill both opposed colonization in the Middle East and supported her plan for an independent Iraq, but progress towards that goal was too slow. As 1919 turned to 1920 Gertrude was getting weaker and Arab unrest, provoked by frustration at the delay of independence and by subversion from Turkey and the Soviet Bolsheviks, was gaining strength. Tribal attacks on British forces brought retaliatory bombing raids by the RAF, and even pro-British sheikhs were growing embittered. Something needed to be done, and when Sir Percy Cox stopped off in Baghdad in June 1920, en route to London, she made one last desperate effort. She had been writing a book-length report on her plans for the future state of Iraq; now she put the finishing touches on it and gave it to Cox to take back to London with him. He did so, and managed to get it presented to Parliament as a white paper. Review of the Civil Administration of Mesopotamia, by Miss Gertrude Bell CBE was one of those rare documents that earned a standing ovation from all sides in the usually quarrelsome House of Commons, and it finally nudged the government into action.

On October 11, 1920, Cox returned to Baghdad as administrator. Days before his arrival, Gertrude and Wilson had an emotional farewell. When he tried to apologize for their poor working relationship she cut him off and told him it was as much her fault as his. That was true on a personal level, but it was generous of her to be so forgiving; she had been working hard to bring about the promised independence, while Wilson had been opposing her every step of the way. Now that obstacle was gone and the road was clear.

CHAPTER 13: THE KINGMAKER

The new country of Iraq – three former Ottoman districts centered around Mosul, Baghdad and Basrah - was a deeply tribal society and British-style parliamentary democracy was never going to work. The nation needed a king and there were two choices. One was the grim fundamentalist Ibn Saud. The other was the Hashemite Faisal bin Hussein Ali al-Hashimi, a leader of the Arab Revolt who was now part of the allied-backed government in Damascus. Hussein had been brought up in Istanbul as a virtual hostage of the Ottomans, and then trained by the Turkish army, but he was an implacable opponent of the empire. When Lawrence met him in October 1916, he marked the young Faisal as a possible leader for the post-war vision that, whatever his faults (and they were many) he shared with Gertrude. Immediately after the war, Lawrence left the Army and went to work for the British foreign office, where he accompanied Faisal to the Paris Peace Conference that formally ended the war. Lawrence had helped install Faisal as King of Syria, but in 1920, France was awarded control over Syria and Faisal was expelled. By the time Cox returned to Baghdad in late 1920, Faisal was living in England. However, he was desperate to return to the Middle East and Cox and Gertrude thought they had the perfect job for them. Young, pro-British and not particularly religious, he seemed like the ideal candidate to unify a country whose biggest divide was between Shia and Sunni Muslims. There was only one problem: most Iraqis had never heard of him. It was time for one last effort by Gertrude.

For six months, she and other British officials toured the country with Faisal, introducing him to them as a potential king. Many of the people were suspicious of the whole idea of nationhood, and some still feared a return of the Ottomans – the Turks had ruled them for five centuries, after all, and it was hard to believe that their empire was gone. Now the trust that Gertrude had built up over years of hard work could make a real difference. She explained that the world had changed, that the Ottoman threat was gone forever. She patiently educated them in what independence would mean. She could also point out their growing prosperity: the economy was swiftly recovering now that the corruption and stagnation of the old regime was gone. There would be more, she promised, if they accepted independence and used it well.

Her efforts worked. In August 1921, the people were given a referendum on independence, and 95 percent of them voted yes. Faisal Hashimi was asked to become king and accepted; on August 23 he was crowned as Faisal I of Iraq. The dedicated group of administrators who had followed the Indian Expeditionary Force north from Basrah had done their job and created a new, independent Arab country. Now, slowly, they began to go home.

But as far as Gertrude was concerned, this was home now. In letters to her parents and to Valentine Chirol she made clear that she no longer missed England.46 On her rare visits to Yorkshire, she slept in the summer house; she knew she had made enemies and didn't want to endanger her family by bringing attackers into their home. Even in Britain she slept with a loaded revolver under her pillow. On the other hand, she was happy in her little Baghdad home, and it was truly hers now – Musa Chalabi, now one of her closest friends, had presented it to her as a gift. Embarrassed, she had still known better to try to refuse a gift from an Arab, so she had made clear that the garden itself was shared. She had done more than anyone else to create a new country. Now she planned to live in it.

And of course, being who she was, she planned to make it better. In 1919, she had been invited to speak at a meeting calling for a public library in Baghdad. By 1921, she was president of the library committee, and three years later the city had a public library, which is now the National Library of Iraq. Next she returned to archaeology, collecting relics of Mesopotamian civilization that dated back to the earliest recorded human cultures and building up the nucleus of what would become the National Museum of Iraq. Although looted during the fall of Saddam Hussein's regime it still has one of the finest collections of ancient artifacts in the world. For decades one of its wings was named after Gertrude, and all exhibits are labeled in both Arabic and English – a practice she began as the Museum's first director.

CONCLUSION

Gertrude Bell died in her home on the night of July 11/12, 1926. She had just recovered from a bout of pleurisy, only to hear that her half-brother Hugo had died of typhoid, and there was a half-empty bottle of sleeping pills beside her bed. An obvious conclusion is suicide brought on by temporary depression. Some have even speculated that she might have been murdered. She certainly did have enemies, both inside and outside Iraq – anyone who holds as much political power as she did has enemies – so murder is a possibility, but a faint one. Suicide is more credible, because she was very attached to Hugo, but if so it must have been a sudden impulse – she had asked her maid to wake her in the morning. The final alternative is an accidental overdose. Perhaps, in her weakened condition, a dose that would normally have been harmless was just too much.

However her life ended, though, it had been a remarkable one. Whatever she set out to do she did with an energy and competence that's little short of awe-inspiring. Whether it was scaling a mountain or building a nation, she was never half-hearted or timid. If Gertrude set out to do something it was almost certain to get done.

Even now, 88 years after her death, there's still debate about her legacy. Some say today's problems in Iraq are caused by the borders she drew, but it's hard to see what she could have done differently. She was faced with a choice between creating a patchwork of states too small to survive, or by risking ethnic conflict somewhere down the line. In fact, until the sectarian violence that was unleashed by Saddam Hussein and his successors, Iraq was remarkably stable by Middle Eastern standards. She knew herself that her boundaries were imperfect, as a look at her writing will show, but she did the best she could. Perhaps the best indicator is how she's viewed in Iraq. After her death most of Baghdad turned out for her funeral; sheikhs travelled from all over the Middle East to be there, and King Faisal watched the procession from his private balcony. When British troops returned to Basrah in 2003 the local population, desperate for proper rule after decades of tyranny, invoked the name of Gertrude Bell. Since the invasion, foreign administrators and advisers have come and gone, and where they weren't detested they've been forgotten. But every week, in Baghdad's old British cemetery, men clean and tidy the immaculate grave of the woman their grandfathers called the Queen of the Desert.

ABOUT LIFECAPS

LifeCaps is an imprint of BookCaps™ Study Guides. With each book, a lesser known or sometimes forgotten life is recapped.

We publish a wide array of topics (from baseball and music to literature and philosophy), so check our growing catalogue regularly (www.bookcaps.com) to see our newest books.

NOTES

[1] The Economist, Sep 7, 2006, *Gertrude of Arabia*
http://www.economist.com/node/7879942

[2] Journal of the Royal Society of Medicine, Nov 2006, *British Maternal Mortality in the 19th and early 20th Centuries*
http://www.ncbi.nlm.nih.gov/pmc/articles/PMC1633559/

[3] Howell, Georgina (2012), *Daughter of the Desert: The Extraordinary Life of Gertrude Bell*

[4] Newcastle University Library, *Gertrude Bell Archive*
http://www.gerty.ncl.ac.uk/

[5] Howell, Georgina (2012), *Daughter of the Desert: The Extraordinary Life of Gertrude Bell*

[6] Howell, Georgina (2012), *Daughter of the Desert: The Extraordinary Life of Gertrude Bell*

[7] Davies & Weaver, *The Dictionary of National Biography 1912-1921,* 1927

[8] Howell, Georgina (2012), *Daughter of the Desert: The Extraordinary Life of Gertrude Bell*

[9] Sweet, Matthew (2001), *Inventing The Victorians*

[10] Sweet, Matthew (2001), *Inventing The Victorians*

[11] Forgotten Newsmakers, *Gertrude Bell (1868-1926)*
http://forgottennewsmakers.com/2011/01/12/gertrude-bell-1868-%E2%80%93-1926-explorer-instrumental-in-founding-iraq/

[12] Howell, Georgina (2012), *Daughter of the Desert: The Extraordinary Life of Gertrude Bell*

[13] *Hafiz*
http://www.hafizonlove.com/bio/index.htm

[14] Howell, Georgina (2012), *Daughter of the Desert: The Extraordinary Life of Gertrude Bell*

[15] Howell, Georgina (2012), *Daughter of the Desert: The Extraordinary Life of Gertrude Bell*

[16] Clark, Ronald (2011), *The Alps*

[17] Howell, Georgina (2012), *Daughter of the Desert: The Extraordinary Life of Gertrude Bell*

[18] Letter, Gertrude Bell to Sir Hugh Bell, August 28, 1899

http://www.gerty.ncl.ac.uk/letter_details.php?letter_id=1071

[19] Letter, Gertrude Bell to Sir Hugh Bell, September 4, 1899

http://www.gerty.ncl.ac.uk/letter_details.php?letter_id=1074

[20] Letter, Gertrude Bell to Sir Hugh Bell, September 4, 1899

http://www.gerty.ncl.ac.uk/letter_details.php?letter_id=1074

[21] Letter, Gertrude Bell to Sir Hugh Bell, August 2, 1900

http://www.gerty.ncl.ac.uk/letter_details.php?letter_id=1215

[22] Letter, Gertrude Bell to Sir Hugh Bell, August 21, 1900

http://www.gerty.ncl.ac.uk/letter_details.php?letter_id=1225

[23] Letter, Gertrude Bell to Sir Hugh Bell, August 25, 1901

http://www.gerty.ncl.ac.uk/letter_details.php?letter_id=1262

[24] Letter, Gertrude Bell to Sir Hugh bell, September 8, 1901

http://www.gerty.ncl.ac.uk/letter_details.php?letter_id=1268

[25] Gertrude Bell's diary, August 4, 1902

http://www.gerty.ncl.ac.uk/diary_details.php?diary_id=221

[26] Howell, Georgina (2012), *Daughter of the Desert: The Extraordinary Life of Gertrude Bell*

[27] Letter, Gertrude Bell to Sir Hugh bell, November 29, 1899

http://www.gerty.ncl.ac.uk/letter_details.php?letter_id=1084

[28] Letter, Gertrude Bell to Florence Bell, December 10, 1899

http://www.gerty.ncl.ac.uk/letter_details.php?letter_id=1090
[29] Letter, Gertrude Bell to Sir Hugh Bell, December 13, 1899

http://www.gerty.ncl.ac.uk/letter_details.php?letter_id=1092
[30] Letter, Gertrude Bell to Florence Bell, February 28, 1900

http://www.gerty.ncl.ac.uk/letter_details.php?letter_id=1129
[31] Letter, Gertrude Bell to Sir Hugh Bell, March 15, 1900

http://www.gerty.ncl.ac.uk/letter_details.php?letter_id=1137
[32] Letter, Gertrude Bell to Sir Hugh Bell, March 25, 1900

http://www.gerty.ncl.ac.uk/letter_details.php?letter_id=1147
[33] Letter, Gertrude Bell to Sir Hugh Bell, May 3, 1900

http://www.gerty.ncl.ac.uk/letter_details.php?letter_id=1177
[34] Letter, Gertrude Bell to Sir Hugh Bell, May 5, 1900

http://www.gerty.ncl.ac.uk/letters.php?year=1900&month=5
[35] Howell, Georgina (2012), *Daughter of the Desert: The Extraordinary Life of Gertrude Bell*
[36] Letter, Gertrude Bell to Sir Hugh Bell, May 16, 1905

http://www.gerty.ncl.ac.uk/letter_details.php?letter_id=1536
[37] Letter, Gertrude Bell to Sir Hugh Bell, July 12, 1907

http://www.gerty.ncl.ac.uk/letter_details.php?letter_id=1613
[38] Letter, Gertrude Bell to Florence Bell, March 17, 1909

http://www.gerty.ncl.ac.uk/letter_details.php?letter_id=1667

[39] Letter, Gertrude Bell to Florence Bell, July 7, 1909

http://www.gerty.ncl.ac.uk/letter_details.php?letter_id=1722
[40] Letter, Gertrude Bell to Sir Hugh Bell, November 29, 1913

http://www.gerty.ncl.ac.uk/letter_details.php?letter_id=20
[41] Letter, Gertrude Bell to Sir Hugh Bell, March 7, 1914

http://www.gerty.ncl.ac.uk/letter_details.php?letter_id=60
[42] Howell, Georgina (2012), *Daughter of the Desert: The Extraordinary Life of Gertrude Bell*
[43] Letter, Gertrude Bell to Florence Bell, November 30, 1915

http://www.gerty.ncl.ac.uk/letter_details.php?letter_id=132
[44] Letter, Gertrude Bell to Sir Hugh Bell, January 24, 1916

http://www.gerty.ncl.ac.uk/letter_details.php?letter_id=145
[45] Howell, Georgina (2012), *Daughter of the Desert: The Extraordinary Life of Gertrude Bell*
[46] Howell, Georgina (2012), *Daughter of the Desert: The Extraordinary Life of Gertrude Bell*

CPSIA information can be obtained
at www.ICGtesting.com
Printed in the USA
LVHW011559230322
714164LV00008B/2118